John & Charles Wesley

Selected Books in the
SkyLight Illuminations Series

John & Charles Wesley

Selections from Their Writings and Hymns—Annotated & Explained

Annotation by Paul Wesley Chilcote, PhD

Walking Together, Finding the Way ®
SKYLIGHT PATHS®
PUBLISHING
Woodstock, Vermont

John & Charles Wesley:
Selections from Their Writings and Hymns—Annotated & Explained

2011 Quality Paperback Edition, First Printing
Introduction, annotations, and back matter © 2011 by Paul Wesley Chilcote

Library of Congress Cataloging-in-Publication Data

John & Charles Wesley : selections from their writings and hymns, annotated & explained / annotation by Paul Wesley Chilcote.
    p. cm. — (SkyLight illuminations)
  "Walking together, finding the way."
  Includes bibliographical references and index.
  ISBN 978-1-59473-309-3 (quality pbk.)
  1. Wesley, John, 1703-1791. 2. Wesley, Charles, 1707–1788. 3. Methodist Church—Doctrines. I. Chilcote, Paul Wesley, 1954– II. Wesley, John, 1703-1791. Selections. 2011. III. Wesley, Charles, 1707–1788. Selections. 2011. IV. Title: John and Charles Wesley.
  BX8495.W5J53 2011
  230'.7—dc23

                                2011027397

10 9 8 7 6 5 4 3 2 1

Cover Design: Walter C. Bumford III, Stockton, Massachusetts
Cover Art: Photograph of stained glass window of the Wesley brothers by Steven Manskar
Manufactured in the United States of America

> SkyLight Paths Publishing is creating a place where people of different spiritual traditions come together for challenge and inspiration, a place where we can help each other understand the mystery that lies at the heart of our existence.
>
> SkyLight Paths sees both believers and seekers as a community that increasingly transcends traditional boundaries of religion and denomination—people wanting to learn from each other, *walking together, finding the way.*®

SkyLight Paths, "Walking Together, Finding the Way" and colophon are trademarks of LongHill Partners, Inc., registered in the U.S. Patent and Trademark Office.

Walking Together, Finding the Way®
Published by SkyLight Paths® Publishing
A Division of LongHill Partners, Inc.
Sunset Farm Offices, Route 4, P.O. Box 237
Woodstock, VT 05091
Tel: (802) 457-4000   Fax: (802) 457-4004
www.skylightpaths.com

For Frank Baker,
my mentor in Wesley studies,
on the 101st anniversary of his birth,
and for all of my students over the years
who have embraced the Wesleyan vision of
faith working by love leading to holiness of heart and life

Contents □

PART TWO
The Triune God of Grace and Love

PART THREE
The Way of Salvation

x **Contents**

PART FIVE
A Compassionate Mission

□ Preface

Just the other day, I overheard someone say that Christianity spreads best through fascination. John and Charles Wesley had a way of making Christianity fascinating again for their time. My hope is that this small collection of their writings ignites the same fascination among readers who turn to this resource for spiritual insight and direction.

A number of rediscoveries triggered this fascination for the Wesleys. First, they introduced a revised vision of God. The Bible that they read proclaimed that God sent Jesus not to condemn the world, but to save it by loving it. This is the God they knew and longed for others to know. Second, once enraptured with this loving God, they created a movement that taught people how to love as they had been loved by Christ. They genuinely believed that love leads inevitably to a union with the One. Third, if disciples were to be fully formed or reshaped in love—into the image of Christ—they had to engage regularly in acts of devotion and worship, compassion, and justice. Only a holistic spirituality could form a holy people. Fourth, the Wesleys were wise enough to know that none of this could be done alone. The experience of God's love compels the community of faith to reach out with glad and generous hearts to all. The communities that the Wesleys formed made room and created safe space for others (hospitality), offered reconciliation and peace to the broken-hearted and the oppressed (healing), and lived in and for God's vision of shalom for all humanity and creation (holiness). I hope their vision fascinates you.

The Wesley brothers were prolific writers. John published over four hundred books, journals, treatises, and pamphlets; Charles wrote over nine thousand hymns and sacred poems. Therefore, I have been unbelievably selective in the process of constructing this anthology. I have tried to stay true to the central emphases of the Wesleyan heritage while collecting some of the great gems of the Wesleys' spiritual teaching. In order to make these eighteenth-century disciples of Jesus more accessible to a contemporary reader, I have found it necessary to edit some of the texts. Language changes continuously and, consequently, some of the terms they used make little sense today. Moreover, the structure of John Wesley's prose can seem tedious to readers today who are more familiar with sound bites than lengthy paragraphs. Whenever I have changed the original, I hope I have not altered the meaning, changed the emphasis, or, in the case of Charles Wesley's poetry in particular, corrupted the fine poetic diction of a lyrical genius. With regard to this process of "translating" older English texts into a more contemporary form, several comments are in order.

In some cases I have simply substituted modern forms for archaic eighteenth-century English conventions. Some of this work was very simple and straightforward. For example, I have translated "quire" into "choir," "burthen'd" into "burdened," and "antient" into "ancient." I have also Americanized typical English spellings, replacing "Saviour," for example, with "Savior." Wherever appropriate, I have replaced "thee" and "thine" with "you" and "your," or have otherwise suitably updated the text. A number of terms that are no longer known or used in the same way called for more radical translation. "Tempers" today means "dispositions," "unfeigned" means "genuine," "vouchsafe" means "give," "withal" can be translated as "regardless," "a little eminence" becomes "a hillside," and while many know what "raiment" means, most today would simply say "clothing." On a number of occasions, I have taken more license with the original text because of major differences in punctuation and sentence structure, most particularly the use of lengthy and complicated clauses.

I am strongly committed to the use of inclusive language in all of my writing and teaching. One of the issues I struggle with is the Wesleys' use of gender-specific language with reference to humanity and God. This distinguishes the age they lived in from our own. Because of Charles

Wesley's frequent use of plural forms and his proclivity for the first person, this is not as large a problem as one might suspect with regard to his hymns. In fact, his gender inclusiveness is quite remarkable on the whole. Wherever I noted possible changes for the purpose of greater inclusivity that were not, in my judgment, destructive to the flow of the text, either prose or poetry, I have made them.

The relational orientation of Wesleyan theology makes it relevant and appealing to many today. People mattered to the Wesleys, and they matter to me. I owe a debt of gratitude to a number of friends and colleagues who have made this volume possible. Nancy Fitzgerald initiated conversation with me about this collection for the SkyLight Illuminations series. She and I had worked together on a few earlier projects. Holding her in great esteem, I never hesitated to move forward with this book under her editorial direction. It would never have come to fruition without her invitation, expert guidance, and ongoing support. I have thoroughly enjoyed working with the editorial staff at SkyLight Paths, especially project editor Lauren Hill and her successor, assistant editor Daniela Cockwill. Several colleagues offered assistance to improve this resource, and I therefore want to express my appreciation to Steve Harper, Randy Maddox, Chuck Yrigoyen, and particularly Ulrike Schuler, who helped me make these texts more accessible to those for whom English is not their first language. One of my students, Rick Hatton, devoted much time and energy to the issue of commentary, identifying the questions he believed would surface in the minds of readers encountering this material for the first time. I am sure that his insights improved my commentary markedly. My wife, Janet, examined the entire manuscript and offered helpful suggestions.

Over the years it has been my joy to introduce students to Wesley texts on three continents at the following institutions: Wesley College in Bristol, England; Boston University School of Theology; St. Paul's United Theological College in Limuru, Kenya; the Methodist Theological School in Ohio; Africa University Faculty of Theology in Old Mutare, Zimbabwe; Garrett-Evangelical Theological Seminary in Evanston, Illinois; the Northwest

House of Theological Studies in Salem, Oregon; Asbury Theological Seminary in Orlando, Florida; Duke Divinity School in Durham, North Carolina; and Ashland Theological Seminary in Ohio. I have dedicated this volume to them and to the remarkable Wesley scholar, Dr. Frank Baker, who directed my path toward the fascinating world of the Wesleys and would have celebrated his 101st birthday as I prepared this volume.

My own roots are deep in the Wesleyan heritage. Despite the fact that I was born into this tradition, I came to embrace it wholeheartedly as my own. John and Charles Wesley are phenomenal mentors in the Christian faith. They still speak to us today with passion and urgency about the great God of love we come to know in Jesus Christ. I hope that their own words awaken a deep sense of wonder, love, and praise in you.

☐ Introduction

John and Charles Wesley represent a bridge between the living traditions of the Christian faith. In their doctrine of salvation, they bridge the gap between popular Roman Catholic and Protestant understandings of redemption, placing equal emphasis on salvation by faith and holy living. Having been strongly influenced by the great theologians of the early church, they emphasize not only the Western concept of forgiveness, but also the Eastern notion of restoration, the forgiven Christian growing ever more fully into the image of Christ. With their emphasis on the centrality and power of the Spirit and their concern for structures that liberate and empower, they provide a paradigm that potentially reconciles historically mainline traditions with the erupting Pentecostal movements in our world today. They afford a profoundly holistic vision of the Christian life that speaks with authenticity and power to postmodern seekers and modern disciples alike. They provide a vision of God that beckons to all those interested in the spiritual life.

Albert Outler, one of the great authorities on John Wesley in the late twentieth century, once claimed that John Wesley had mastered the art of plastic synthesis; both brothers were able to hold together aspects of Christian faith and practice often split apart by the followers of Jesus in every age. They taught and practiced a form of Christian discipleship that held together faith and works, personal and social holiness, physical and spiritual concerns, works of piety and works of mercy, Christianity and culture. They preached and sang a "practical divinity" that touched people where they lived, inspired them to be the children of God they were created to be, and immersed their followers in time-honored spiritual practices that liberated and empowered those who were often on the margins

1

of life. Their vision was ancient, biblical, practical, and timely; their teachings and writings remain vital, dynamic, meaningful, and relevant today.

As devout priests of the Church of England to their dying days, the Wesley brothers fully embraced their Anglican roots. Despite the fact that their movement—Methodism—eventually separated after their deaths from the institutional church they loved, the essence of that English Christian tradition shaped them, perhaps more than any other single force. The Church of England represented, for them, a heritage of continuity that reached back into the earliest beginnings of Christianity. It helped them feel connected to the great cloud of witnesses, to the apostles and martyrs and saints who preceded them in faith over the centuries. It provided a perennial reminder to them that the family of God—the truly catholic or universal church—is always much larger than any of us can see or comprehend. The Wesleys understood the church to be a community, a communion of faith through the ages, a corporate body that connects us to God and one another through time and space.

A confluence of many factors and forces beyond their native Anglicanism, however, molded John and Charles Wesley into the men they would become—men dedicated to God above all things. The parents of the brothers both had converted to the Church of England in their teen years from the independent Puritan churches in which they had been raised. Both Samuel and Susanna Wesley had drunk deeply from the wells of the Puritan heritage and carried its ethos into the home in which they raised their family. They loved the primitive church and the spirituality of the earliest Christian communities reflected in the pages of the Christian Scriptures. They appreciated the simplicity of life and worship for which the Puritans longed, and the holiness of life, or purity, from which they took their name. The Wesley home combined some of the thought and practice of English Puritanism with the traditions and heritage of the Church of England. The mature spirituality of the Wesleys combined an Anglican holiness of intent—the desire to please God in all things—and a Puritan interior assurance—the sense of abiding in God's favor. Above all else, this conjunction of English traditions established a "both/and" paradigm—that synthetic approach to both theology and life to which Outler referred. Not surprisingly, John, in particular, was always seeking third alternatives through which to articulate and live his faith over against the divisive polarities of his age; he offers a methodology that may apply to our time as well.

Two other movements greatly influenced the Wesleys: Continental Pietism and Eastern Orthodoxy. Pietism stressed the importance of "heart religion." Born into an age that would witness the flowering of "The Enlightenment," with its emphasis on reason and scientific certainty, the Wesleys found in the Pietist theologians and practitioners (men like Philipp Jakob Spener and August Hermann Francke of the University of Halle in Germany) an important counterbalance to the arid and detached Deism that tended to dominate the religious intelligentsia of their day. The Deists sought to apply the rationalistic principles of the day to the Christian religion, accepting only what was reasonable in its teachings and practice. From the Pietists the Wesleys learned the importance of growth in grace made possible through the intimacy of small groups. The brothers adopted the Continental model of the "little church within the church" and developed their own network of "societies" with band and class meetings to meet the spiritual needs of their followers. These structures became the hallmark of the Methodist movement. The Pietist emphasis on the dynamic nature of faith—the faith "by which," not simply "in which," one believes—warmed the hearts of the Wesleys. Although doctrine played a critical role in the development of Methodism, the Wesleys consistently elevated the credibility of the Christian lifestyle above purity in matters of Christian thought.

From the early church fathers, the Wesleys developed an equally dynamic vision of the goal of the Christian life. They were strongly attracted to an Eastern Orthodox understanding of salvation as the restoration of the image of God among those who participated in Christ. Their view of redemption rested firmly on a robust conception of faith as trust in the

Christ who forgives, but they believed as well in an equally dynamic conception of holiness—the fullest possible love of God and neighbor as the goal of the Christian life. They combined a Protestant foundation with an Orthodox (even Catholic) goal—the vision of a fully sanctified life. They appreciated the conception of mystery in the Orthodox tradition, the cosmic nature of God's purpose and mission, and a spirituality that revolved around the celebration of Holy Communion. They rooted their lives in Western practices of prayer, embraced the practical mysticism of the late medieval church, and promoted a semimonastic rule of life among their followers. The amazing confluence of these various streams can be seen most fully in the lives and ministries of these two men of God.

A Brief Overview of the Wesleys' Lives

Born at the beginning of the eighteenth century at Epworth in Lincolnshire in the northeast of England, John on June 17, 1703, and Charles on December 18, 1707, these two boys were among the lucky ones to make it through the early years of life. Of their probable seventeen siblings, only Samuel, the firstborn of the family, and seven of the girls survived into adulthood. Three particular events or concerns related to these Epworth years had a lasting influence on John and Charles Wesley. In 1709 the Epworth rectory, the parsonage for St. Andrew's parish church where their father served as priest, was completely demolished by a fire. John was five years old, his younger brother, Charles, just a year and a half. Young John's dramatic rescue from the fire became the center of the story as it was retold over the years. Susanna, in particular, saw the fiery rescue as a sign from God concerning the importance of her young "Jacky." In later years, John adopted for himself the biblical phrase "a brand plucked from the burning," establishing this event as a part of Methodist legend.

A second event is of equal importance. During one of Samuel's many absences, in 1712, Susanna set up a house meeting in the rectory kitchen to supplement the poor spiritual leadership of the young priest Samuel had hired in his stead. Initially intended just for her family, these spiritual gatherings began to attract servants, parishioners, and neigh-bors. Eventually, as many as two hundred gathered to take advantage of her spiritual wisdom and guidance. These meetings were conducted on Sunday evenings and expanded over time into something approaching services of worship. When criticized for this practice, Susanna aptly defended her actions, both to the community and to her husband. These kitchen services imprinted two important lessons on the impressionable minds of Susanna's sons. First, nothing is more important than the con-science void of offense to God. One must do what one feels called to do. Second, women have an important place and role in the community of faith. It is largely owing to Susanna's influence that John seldom wavered in his conviction that no one—not even a woman—ought to be prohibited from doing God's work in obedience to the inner calling of her conscience.

The third area of concern has to do with the interest of both Samuel and Susanna in the development of so-called "Societies" in their day. Susanna's kitchen meetings, in fact, may have been influenced by her knowledge of this movement. The society that drew Samuel's attention more than any other was the Society for Promoting Christian Knowledge, or the SPCK. In 1700 he had attempted to set up a small religious society in Epworth built upon the model of the developing societies in London. The parallel between the design of the religious societies of Epworth—the purpose of which was the promotion of real holiness of heart and life—and the Methodist Societies founded by John and Charles some three decades later are unmistakable.

In 1714, at eleven years of age, John was sent by his parents to the Charterhouse in London to continue his education, the Duke of Bucking-hamshire having nominated him as a foundation scholar. Little is known about this time in his life, but he seems to have coped with his new envi-ronment, devoting himself closely to his studies. Two years later, in 1716, at the young age of eight, Charles was sent to Westminster School, also in London, where he spent the next ten years of his life. While John was alone at Charterhouse, Charles enjoyed the watchful care of his older brother, Samuel, with whom he even shared lodging, at least for his first five years. The discipline in these schools was severe; if these schools toughened the boys, it did not coarsen them. Both schools had reputations for being places of learning and strict discipline. They prepared the boys well for later studies at Christ Church, Oxford, where John matriculated in 1720 and Charles in 1726. A new chapter in both their lives awaited them there.

John Wesley later described developments during the Oxford years (1720–1735) as the "first rise of Methodism." Although Charles frequently led the way in many of the personal and institutional developments that revolved around this rising evangelical revival within the church, he generally deferred to his older brother in terms of leadership. At the university, for example, Charles founded a so-called "Holy Club," a loosely associated group of students who devoted themselves to disciplined piety and social service. They studied the Bible, prayed together, visited prisons, engaged in ministries among the poor, and regularly received Eucharist in an effort to practice holy living. They were encouraged in this methodical discipleship by reading classic devotional texts such as Jeremy Taylor's *Rules and Exercises of Holy Living and Dying*, Thomas à Kempis's *The Imitation of Christ*, and William Law's *Serious Call to a Devout and Holy Life*. It was not long before their detractors labeled them "Methodists." This whole experience birthed a vision of accountable discipleship in the hearts and minds of the Wesleys, an understanding of the Christian life that combined vital piety and sound learning, disciplined practice and social witness, all within the context of supportive small groups.

The "second rise of Methodism" relates to the brief period that John and Charles served as missionaries in the American colonies (1736–1738). By the time the brothers set sail for Georgia in November 1735, both were ordained priests. They responded to a call to provide spiritual leadership in General Oglethorpe's experimental colony and hoped to share the good news of the gospel with the "noble savages," an aspect of their quest to rediscover "primitive Christianity." Despite the fact that they hardly realized any of their dreams, the most significant aspect of this period was quite simply their introduction to the Moravians. The Wesleys were particularly impressed with these Lutheran Pietists from Germany who accompanied them on their treacherous journey across the Atlantic Ocean. During several horrendous storms, these faithful Christian people remained calm and at peace despite the constant threat of death. Their faith—a confident trust in the risen Lord—challenged the Wesleys' own vision of Christian rectitude and holy living at that time, and made them consider seriously the foundation on which they had built their lives. Of particular interest to them was the Moravian conviction that love transcends obedience to rules. The Moravians believed that Christians could live in the assurance that they were children of God, despite their failure to measure up to the godly disciplines that defined their lives.

The Wesleys returned to England somewhat bewildered, Charles first in December 1736 and John in February 1738. Their final and decisive Moravian influence was Peter Böhler, a German-born Moravian missionary who functioned as something of a spiritual guide for both brothers during the early months of 1738. The central issue that Böhler pressed on them was their lack of faith, despite the fact that they had been religious men, even devout followers of Jesus. What remained unclear to the Wesleys was exactly what kind of faith their Moravian friend was advocating and how they could ever experience it. The "third rise of Methodism," then, involved their establishment of the Fetter Lane Society, a small, supportive community of the faithful in which to explore this very question, and other accountability groups in London as well. The stage was set for the brothers to experience the inner trust and reliance on God that they sought.

Charles experienced God's unconditional love in a "religious experience" on May 21, 1738, that preceded the famous "Aldersgate Experience" of his older brother, John, three days later. No excerpt from the Wesleyan corpus is better known, perhaps, than John's account of this "heartwarming" event. At a small gathering of devout Christians at Aldersgate Street in London, John felt his sins forgiven through Jesus and experienced an intimacy with God, as his brother had just days before, that he had never known. The legendary quality of Aldersgate has led to two opposite dangers in the Methodist tradition, however, to either undervalue this "conversion" in relation to earlier religious experiences or to overvalue it by denigrating what had gone before and thereby isolating it from other formative events.

One such event of monumental proportion followed in April 1739 and can be described as the genuine birth of the Methodist revival. Responding to the clarion call of his friend and colleague, George Whitefield, on March 29, 1739, John set out for Bristol, anticipating that he might find himself overtaken by innovative developments there. On April 2, he recorded the events that transpired: "I submitted to be more vile, and proclaimed in the highways the glad tidings of salvation, speaking from a little eminence in a ground adjoining to the city, to about three thousand people." This was his very first venture into "field preaching," and he could hardly have anticipated the spiritual fruit that it would produce. His text that day was appropriate. "The Spirit of the Lord is upon me, because he hath anointed me to preach the gospel to the poor; he hath sent me to heal the brokenhearted, to preach deliverance to the captives, and recovering of sight to the blind, to set at liberty them that are bruised, to preach the acceptable year of the Lord" (Luke 4:18–19 KJV). Those who responded to his preaching were soon organized into small groups, or Societies, under his spiritual direction, and one of the most significant revivals in Christian history ensued.

Throughout the remainder of their lives, the Wesley brothers remained inextricably bound to this movement; their theology shaped the movement, and Methodism shaped their spirituality. The lives of these leaders reflect the contours of the important developments within the movement, conventionally divided into four main phases. The first decade (1739–1749) was, by far, the most decisive. The Wesleys organized a network of Societies, divided into yet smaller groups of bands (four to seven) and classes (twelve). These structures for accountable discipleship liberated those awakened by the experience of God's grace, engendered faith, and provided nurture for growth in grace and love. During these years the Wesleys held the first conference for their expanding band of itinerant preachers, built their first meetinghouse, and defended their movement against the charge of "enthusiasm." In its second decade (1749–1759), Methodism established its identity as an "evangelistic order" within the Church of England. At the beginning of this period, Charles married Sarah Gwynn, settled in Bristol, and began to raise his family, staying intimately connected to the movement nonetheless. The Wesleys had stressed "holiness of heart and life" from the outset, but developments during the third decade (1759–1769) led them to urge the importance of the fullest possible love of God and love of neighbor all the more.

The final score of years from 1769 was filled with turmoil and triumph. Controversy sharpened Wesleyan theology. Against the Calvinist doctrine of predestination, which emphasized God's unilateral choice of those who would be saved or damned, the Wesleys promoted a dynamic understanding of salvation that embraced both divine initiative and human responsibility. John wrote with passion against the rebellion of the American colonies (stirring up quite a bit of resentment on the western side of the Atlantic). He preached vehemently against slavery, an abomination described by him in the very last letter he ever wrote as the "execrable sum of all villainies." The brothers themselves locked horns over John's action to provide spiritual leadership for his burgeoning movement in the United States by "ordaining" men for service there in 1784, thereby signaling to some an inevitable split from the parent church. The astronomical growth of the Methodist Societies in Britain required John to draw on all his formidable gifts as an administrator without peer. But success even proved to be one of the Wesleys' greatest challenges as Methodists toward the end of the century tended to embrace their newfound social status and abandoned their first love—Jesus' gospel to the poor. Following a lifetime of service to God and neighbor, Charles Wesley preceded his older brother in death on March 29, 1788; John died in London on March 2, 1791.

By the beginning of the nineteenth century, Methodist membership was approaching one hundred thousand. More than three hundred itinerant, or traveling, preachers provided spiritual leadership for the hundreds of Methodist Societies divided into nearly eighty circuits and some four hundred chapels. John left a doctrinal standard for Methodism in his published *Sermons* and his *Explanatory Notes upon the New Testament*; Charles left the informal standard of doctrine and spirituality expressed in the 1780 *Collection of Hymns for the Use of the People Called Methodists*. Truth be told, these works represent the tip of the iceberg in terms of their stupendous literary output.

The Wesleys' Literary Output

Charles Wesley's Hymns

Charles's primary gift to the world was the production of some 9,000 hymns and sacred poems through which the vast majority of people called Methodists learned their theology. According to the greatest Wesley historian of the twentieth century, Frank Baker, he wrote approximately 180,000 lines of poetry and 27,000 stanzas, producing, on average, about 180 hymns per year. It is not too much to say that Methodism was born in the song of this amazing hymn writer. In the early years of the revival, it was not uncommon for him to preach in the open air to a spellbound crowd gathered by his rich voice singing one of his own hymns.

The blossoming of his evangelical hymns began in 1739 with the advent of three successive editions of *Hymns and Sacred Poems*, jointly published with his brother John. But Charles also produced hymn collections on various themes, including *Hymns on the Trinity, Funeral Hymns, Hymns for Children*, and *Hymns for the Christian Family*, or the great festivals of the Christian year: *Hymns for the Nativity of Our Lord, Hymns for Our Lord's Resurrection, Hymns for Ascension-Day*, and *Hymns for Whit-Sunday* (or Pentecost). In 1749 he published his first hymn book in anticipation of his marriage, and independent of his brother's influence, a two-volume collection of *Hymns and Sacred Poems*. In many of his lyrical works he addressed practical, spiritual questions, producing hymns for backsliders, hymns for times of trouble, and hymns for prisoners, always emphasizing God's everlasting love. There was scarcely an arena of Christian belief, observance, or behavior that Charles did not address in his poetry.

During a lengthy period of illness in 1762, he worked his way through the Bible systematically and published *Short Hymns on Select Passages of the Holy Scriptures*—2,349 poems that function as a biblical commentary in poetry, a lyrical paraphrase of scripture. This collection remains one of the most extensive poetical and devotional commentaries on the Bible. His 166 *Hymns on the Lord's Supper*, a joint venture with John, demonstrated the centrality of the Eucharist to their spirituality. While technically published by his brother John, the 1780 *Collection of Hymns*, including more than 500 of Charles's own compositions, stands out as one of the most significant hymn books in the history of the church. For many years this collection provided the standard poetic explication of virtually every dimension of Methodist teaching—it is the compilation of Charles's lyrical theology.

To this amazing body of hymnody we must add Charles's sermons and journal. Only recently collected in a definitive edition, the small sermon corpus reflects Wesley's concern with communicating scriptural truth effectively beyond his poetic medium. His journal, while revealing important insights about his life and work, is far from complete, with major gaps, some in the most crucial periods of his life. I have drawn on very little of this material in the construction of this volume, relying almost exclusively on the hymns.

John Wesley's Writings

John Wesley published more than 450 separate items in the course of his life, ranging from brief pamphlets like his eleven-page *Thoughts on a Single Life* (1765) to full-blown theological treatises, the lengthiest of which was his explication of *The Doctrine of Original Sin* (1757). Many of his published works went through multiple editions during his lifetime; he prepared, for example, eleven editions of the tract *The Character of a*

Methodist (1742), and the primary guidebook for his movement, *The Nature, Design, and General Rules of Our United Societies*, published originally the following year, saw no fewer than twenty-one editions. He published carefully redacted editions of other authors' writings, such as Thomas à Kempis's *Imitation of Christ* (retitled *The Christian's Pattern*), but whatever he published bore his unique stamp. His first book, *A Collection of Forms of Prayer for Every Day of the Week*, he produced while still a fellow of Lincoln College at Oxford in 1733. Thirty-one volumes of the definitive edition of *The Works of John Wesley*, a monumental scholarly project still under production, are divided into eleven basic categories: *Sermons on Several Occasions* (four volumes); *Explanatory Notes upon the New Testament* (two volumes); the 1780 *Collection of Hymns*; *Prayers Private and Public*; *The Methodist Societies* (two volumes); *Doctrinal Writings* (three volumes); *Pastoral, Ethical, and Instructional Writings*; *Natural Philosophy and Medicine*; *Editorial Works*; *Journals and Diaries* (seven volumes); and *Letters* (seven volumes).

SERMONS

John Wesley was one of the greatest preachers of all time, preaching no fewer than forty thousand sermons throughout the course of his sixty-six-year ministry. In order for others to better understand his movement, and to explain more fully to his followers exactly what he believed, he began to publish his sermons. He published four volumes of *Sermons on Several Occasions* from 1746 to 1760. The forty-four sermons contained in these volumes functioned as a distinctive "doctrinal standard" for the Methodist people. Nine sermons were later added to the original forty-four in order to clarify some points and to address some new issues. While these additional sermons were never given the same authoritative status as the original collection, they were important to the early Methodists. John wrote all of these sermons except for Sermon III, "Awake, Thou That Sleepest," which his brother Charles had preached at Oxford University.

It might seem strange, but John Wesley did not preach all of the sermons he published. In fact, the published sermons were really intended more for reading in the context of private study than for hearing in a setting of public worship. They are more like "sermonic essays." Eyewitness accounts confirm that Wesley's actual preaching was very different in form, if not in substance, from these written essays. He very seldom preached, for example, from a prepared manuscript, preferring to speak spontaneously "from the heart." Every sermon, in one way or another, called for a gracious response to God's grace, lived out in a real world. Wesley's published sermons, likewise, were both theological and practical. In one of the prefaces to his sermons, Wesley says that he has intentionally used "plain words for plain people." The standard sermons, many excerpts from which are included in this volume, are variations on the theme of the Wesleys' distinctive understanding of salvation. They emphasize the centrality of grace, the view of faith as pardon and reconciliation, and the assurance of God's mercy confirmed by the Spirit of Jesus. They describe the way God works in the lives of faithful people to make them whole. The "law of love," revealed in the life, death, and resurrection of Jesus, defines the essence of what it means to be a Christian. It is noteworthy that no fewer than thirteen of these sermons are Wesley's reflections on Jesus' Sermon on the Mount. The sermons are all about God's grace and the fullness of God's grace in our lives.

THEOLOGICAL TRACTS AND TREATISES

The number and variety of John Wesley's theological writings comprise a nearly insurmountable bulk of material. A collection of excerpted material such as this provides something like an index of Wesley's thought. While the sermons serve as the primary window into the theology and spirituality of the Wesleyan heritage, a number of the other theological writings provide balance and perspective. Like Augustine, much of John's theology was hammered out on the anvil of controversy and over against competing theological positions. In his various *Appeals to Men of Reason and Religion*, begun in 1743, for example, Wesley sought to mitigate theological tensions within the Church of England, presenting the first defense of his own doctrinal emphases. In tracts like *A Dialogue between a Predestinarian and His Friend* (1741), *Predestination Calmly Considered* (1752), and *Thoughts upon Necessity* (1774), he battles the perennial nemesis of Calvinistic determinism, the view that God has already determined who will or will not be saved. His *Letter to a Person Lately Join'd with the People Call'd Quakers* (1748) functions much like an olive branch held out in one direction, while his *Letter to a Roman Catholick* (1749) extends the hand of fellowship in the other, with these circular letters pointing out both the similarities and the differences between these widely divergent traditions and his own movement. Despite the fact that Wesley was not a systematic theologian, his theology was coherent and cohesive.

Most of the theological writings that appear here to balance the sermons could be categorized as apologetic writings—in other words, publications in which Wesley sought to defend his theology against his opponents. Three stand out: *The Character of a Methodist* (1742) and *A Plain Account of the People Called Methodists* (1749), both of which attempt to portray Methodists as authentic Christians, and *A Plain Account of Christian Perfection* (1766), arguably John Wesley's magnum opus. "Christian perfection" was the single most consistent theme in Wesley's life and thought and one of the most important distinguishing marks of the Methodist movement. On one occasion he referred to this doctrine as "the grand depositum which God has lodged with the people called Methodists; and for the sake of propagating this chiefly He appeared to have raised us up" (letter to Robert Carr Brackenbury, September 15, 1790). In 1766 Wesley published this full-blown treatise in which he collected extracts from almost all he had ever written or said on the subject, and wove them into a sort of cumulative exposition, stressing the continuity of his thought and centrality of this doctrine.

JOURNALS AND LETTERS

John Wesley began keeping a journal in 1725, a practice he maintained almost until his dying day. This amazing record of his life provides a wide-angled mirror not only of his own life, but also of the time in which he lived. It stands now as a classic in English literature, even rivaling the famous diary of Samuel Pepys. At first appearances, the journal might seem quite straightforward, but it is actually an extremely complicated document. The complexity arises from the fact that John maintained a journal on multiple levels. He kept a daily diary—an abbreviated, shorthand, and sometimes cipher account of every day of his life. This he expanded into a narrative manuscript journal, excerpts of which, in addition to other autobiographical material and letters, he then published for the purpose of public consumption as so-called *Extracts of the Journal*. Like his apologetical writings, this form of the journal also functioned to defend his actions and movement in addition to inspiring and teaching his followers. The "Standard Edition" of the journal, edited by Nehemiah Curnock in the early twentieth century, filled eight volumes; the definitive edition, now complete, comprises volumes 18–24 of *The Works of John Wesley*. The eighteenth century was an age of correspondence. The parallel "Standard Edition" of John's letters, published by John Telford in 1931, directly paralleled Curnock's eight volumes. The modern definitive edition of this collection is still in production and will comprise seven volumes. Given the constraints of this anthology, unfortunately, little of this material can be included here.

This vast array of written work, amounting to millions of words, from hymns to sermons, from treatises to journals, reveals the depth of John and Charles Wesley's spirituality and the serious nature of their theology. I have drawn on as many of the Wesleys' writings as possible that were suitable for an introductory anthology such as this.

Salient Themes in Wesleyan Theology and Spirituality

The salient themes in Wesleyan theology and spirituality include the foundation of the grace and love of God, the way of salvation, accountable discipleship in a community of grace, and compassionate mission in God's world.

The Triune God of Grace and Love

The Wesleys built their theology and spirituality on the foundation of grace. In his sermon "On Working Out Our Own Salvation," John talks about two grand heads of doctrine. The first is grace as it pertains to the work of God *for us* in Jesus; the second is grace as it pertains to the work of God *in us* through the power of the Holy Spirit. John and Charles draw an intimate connection between this grace and the loving God known to us as Father, Son, and Holy Spirit. For the Wesleys, grace is a relational term with which to talk about love, a word that embraces the full image of God, creation, and humankind. This expansive understanding of love and grace links theology and practice—our thoughts about God and our actions. God's gracious love holds everything together and gives meaning and purpose to all created things. In his well-known hymn, "Love Divine, All Loves Excelling," Charles speaks of God as "pure, unbounded love." The goal of life is to be filled with this love.

The Wesleys understood the Christian life, therefore, as a pilgrimage of "grace upon grace." The practice of Christianity begins in grace, grows in grace, and finds its ultimate completion in God's grace. Grace is God's unmerited love, restoring our relationship to God and renewing God's own image in our lives. Through grace, God leads us into a dance of joy, justice, and jubilee in which we seek to radiate God's love, participate in God's reign, and seek the restoration of all things in the Three-One God. Christian discipleship is, first and foremost, a grace-filled response to the free gift of God's all-sufficient grace.

The Way of Salvation

In Martin Luther's theology of the cross, the cross of Jesus functions as the focal point. The axial theme of John Calvin's theology is divine sovereignty— God's gracious rule over all dimensions of life. The Wesleys constructed a theology oriented essentially around soteriology, or the doctrine of salvation. The so-called Wesleyan "way of salvation" consists essentially of three dynamic movements: repentance, faith, and holiness.

Repentance. John Wesley defined repentance as a true self-understanding akin to that experienced by the prodigal son who "came to himself" in the realization that he was far from his true home. The essence of repentance is to place oneself before God, to experience the gaping chasm that separates the sinful creature from the Creator, but to find in God the One who is also close at hand and truly loves. Because God is a God who seeks to restore all things and is a God of mercy and love, the movement from repentance to faith, the Wesleys believed, is but a step.

Faith. Faith has to do with the capacity to entrust one's life fully to God. Drawing on the teachings of their Anglican heritage, John and Charles both defined saving faith as a genuine trust and confidence in the mercy and love of God through Jesus and a steadfast hope of all good things at God's hand. The center around which all else revolved for the Methodists was the shared experience of faith-as-trust and salvation by grace. The more John preached and Charles sang this gospel through his hymns, the more people experienced spiritual liberation in their lives.

Holiness. Holiness is a shorthand term for the whole process by which God restores Christlike love in our lives. While justification by grace through faith is the foundation of the Christian life, holiness of heart and life, or sanctification, is the process that leads to the ultimate goal of perfect love. The Wesleyan concept of salvation can be encapsulated in the phrase "faith working by love leading to holiness of heart and life." John Wesley used the term "Christian perfection" to describe the goal: the fullest possible love of God and neighbor. Because this was such a central doctrine in the Wesleyan movement, it demands a somewhat fuller explication. This concept of Christian perfection can be summarized in seven basic points:

(1) *Love.* Christian perfection is the fullest possible love of God and neighbor—no less, but also no more.

(2) *Purity of Intention*. The essence of Christian perfection is purity of intention, that is, seeking to please God in all thought, word, and action.

(3) *The Definition of Sin*. Christian perfection is freedom from sin "properly-so-called," that is, "a voluntary transgression of a known law." It is the power not to sin willfully and its concomitant freedom from the tyranny of evil.

(4) *Immediacy*. Despite the fact that Wesley thought the gift of perfect love was normally given at the point of death, he was adamant on the point that if perfection is a possibility at all, it must at least be possible in the span of human life.

(5) *Dynamism*. Wesley's basic conception of perfection in the Christian life was dynamic, not static, in nature. He assumed that growth in holiness would continue within Christian perfection and not just before it.

(6) *Restoration*. Wesley looked to the early church and its understanding of salvation as the restoration of the image of God for his doctrine of Christian perfection. It means essentially conformity to Jesus in all things, the believer perennially dependent on God for whatever level of restoration is made possible through the gracious power of the Holy Spirit.

(7) *Happiness*. Holiness is happiness. The fullest expression of holiness in life was the truest form of happiness. The goal of the Christian life, therefore, was essentially "a blessed abiding" in God. The Beatitudes (Matthew 5:3–12) summarize the Wesleyan conception of Christian perfection.

A Community of Grace

In defense of his expanding network of Methodist Societies, John Wesley identified small groups as the distinguishing mark of the movement. In addition to organizing a network of itinerant preacher/evangelists, he and

Charles built up a structure to sustain that ministry and in which his follow-ers were encouraged to "watch over one another in love." The character of these communities, their embodiment of a holistic spirituality, and the central place of the Sacrament of Holy Communion within them shaped the early Methodist people in remarkable ways.

The Character of Community. The Wesleys developed the first Societies in Bristol initially as small groups that met weekly for worship, fellowship, prayer, and instruction. Mutual encouragement and genuine care marked these groups as places of support for those who sought to become loving disciples of Jesus. Leaders in these groups had to be persons of spiritual and emotional maturity. Class and band meetings provided an opportu-nity not only to connect with one another but also to commune with God through the intimacy of this fellowship. They were laboratories in which Wesleyan practices such as self-denial, transparency, simplicity, hospitality, and generosity were discussed and nurtured. In the intimacy of these small groups, the early Methodists learned what it meant to grow in Jesus and, together, they plumbed the depths of God's love for them all. Above all, they cultivated a holistic spirituality that combined works of piety and works of mercy.

Holistic Spirituality. Fellowship in small groups was just one "means of grace" in a constellation of spiritual practices or disciplines, the purpose of which was richer communion with God through Christ. In addition to Christian fellowship, or conference, John Wesley also included prayer and fasting, Bible study, and participation in the Sacrament of Holy Commu-nion among the "instituted means of grace." He called these "works of piety." Unlike many Christian movements prior to and after the Wesleyan revival, the Wesleys found it impossible to separate their personal experi-ence of God and devotion to the risen Lord from their active role as agents of reconciliation and social transformation in the world. To the various works of piety, therefore, they added "works of mercy," included among the more expansive "prudential means of grace." The first two of the three "General Rules" enjoined the Methodists to "avoid evil" and to "do good," a rather simple and straightforward philosophy of life. Authentic Christianity, they believed, consists of a constant inward and outward movement. The combination of these practices nurtured and sustained the early Methodists and also provided the energy that fueled the Wesleyan movement as a powerful religious awakening.

Eucharistic Life. The Wesleyan revival was both "evangelical" (a rediscovery of God's word of grace) and "eucharistic" (a rediscovery of the Sacrament of Holy Communion as a way to experience that grace). The Wesleys believed that sacramental grace and evangelical experience are necessary counterparts in both worship and the Christian life. The celebration of the Lord's Supper shaped their understanding of God's love for them and their reciprocal love for God, all powerfully symbolized for them in the sharing of a meal. The Sacrament not only enabled the Wesleys to remember the past event of the cross and Jesus' redemptive work for all, but it also helped them celebrate the presence of the living Lord in a feast of thanksgiving and oriented their communities in hope toward the future consummation of all things in the great heavenly banquet to come. Charles Wesley's hymns provided lyrical theological reflections on these themes related to the Sacrament as a memorial, a sign and means of grace, and a pledge of heaven.

A Compassionate Mission

In their own day, the Wesleys rediscovered what is often described today as a missional church—a community of faith that reaches out to others intentionally to demonstrate the way of Jesus. A robust theological foundation undergirded the missional vision that gave birth to their movement of spiritual renewal. The missional practices of the Wesleys mirrored their understanding of a God who was primarily missional in nature, always reaching out to others with love. Moreover, they firmly believed that God was active and at work in the world to save and restore all creation, to bring about the new creation promised in scripture. These primary convictions led the Wesleys to reclaim mission as the church's reason for being and evangelism as the heart of that mission in the world. They developed a holistic vision of mission and evangelism that refused to separate faith and works, personal salvation and social justice, physical and spiritual needs.

To use a phrase coined by twentieth-century Lutheran theologian and martyr Dietrich Bonhoeffer, the Wesleys believed that God calls the community of faith to be "a church for others." Although mission belongs properly to God, the Wesleys believed that all people have the privilege of participating in God's mission through their own proclamation and embodiment of the good news of God's love in Christ. In the same way that God entered human history and took on flesh in the person of Jesus, the Wesleys sought to live incarnationally by investing themselves in the lives of God's children wherever they found them. Charles Wesley used a powerful image to communicate this understanding of mission and God's call to be "gospel-bearers." He described the Christian as a "transcript of the Trinity." This means essentially that God writes God's self into our very being so that when other people "read" our lives, they perceive God and experience God's love through us. Genuine Christians serve the present age by giving their lives for the life of God's world.

John and Charles Wesley went to great lengths to specify the character of this service. First, Christian servants simply offer to others what they have freely received from God. Because they have encountered the ultimate good news of God's love in Jesus and received the peace that gift affords, they engage in evangelism—offering God's grace to all in word and deed. Moreover, to have the mind of Christ, for them, meant to care for the poor. A disciple with a living faith is the one whose whole heart has been renewed, who longs to radiate the whole image of God in his or her life and therefore hears the cry of the poor and wills, with God, that all should truly live. So John preached resolutely against the sin of African slavery, offered plans to ameliorate human poverty and hunger, and advocated for the rights of women in his day. The Wesleyan vision of mission, thus understood, was *a life* to be lived, not just an act. It united piety and mercy, worship and compassion, prayer and justice. It involved a humble walk with the Lord, lived out daily in kindness and justice, healing those who were sick, liberating those who were oppressed, empowering those who stood on the margins of life, and caring for the poor.

The Wesleys embraced a radical vision of God's activity in the world and lived in hope of the realization of God's own vision of shalom (peace). The theme of "new creation" pervades their writings. In his *Explanatory Notes upon the New Testament*, John Wesley actually deviated from the authorized translation of 2 Corinthians 5:17, "Therefore if any man be in Christ, he is a *new creature*," and suggested this much more expansive vision: "Therefore if anyone be in Christ, there is a new creation." The Wesleys believed that God called the church to be a sign of this new creation, a community in which all those things that separate people are bridged at the table of the Lord. They sought to stand in the juncture, as it were, between the old world that is passing away and the new world that is being birthed in Christ—despite all appearances. Without minimizing the importance of personal conversion, they expanded the horizon of the early Methodist people to embrace the larger vision of God's shalom. John, in particular, encapsulated this vision in the word *benevolence*. This practice consisted in all efforts to realize God's shalom in the life of the world, to embody the peaceable kingdom.

The Wesleyan Legacy

John and Charles Wesley influenced Christian thought and practice more than most people realize. Every age needs winsome spiritual mentors. In the current era of religionless spirituality often fixated on self-actualization, the Wesleyan heritage affords a different vision of existence—a life of discipleship rooted in Jesus that points to an alternative way of being in the world for the sake of love. The Wesley brothers lived in and for this vision; they embodied faith, working by love, leading to holiness of heart and life. Since the middle of the twentieth century there has been something of a renaissance in Wesley studies. The dynamic nature of their Christian vision of redemption, discipleship, and mission and their embrace of all who seek to serve Jesus by serving others in the world stand in stark contrast to judgmental and exclusivist traditions that cast a shadow over genuine Christianity. The Wesleyan practices of hospitality, healing, and holiness attract all who seek to find abundant life in the service of love. At least six elements comprise the Wesleys' living legacy.

Commitment. From their parents, John and Charles Wesley learned the importance of wholehearted dedication to God. There could be no half measures for them. One of the greatest dangers to the Christian faith, as the title of John's sermon, "The Almost Christian," indicates, is anything that falls short of full commitment. God gave us God's all; we are called to offer back the whole of ourselves—all we are and all we have—as a living sacrifice to God.

Orthodoxy. We generally think of orthodoxy as "right belief," but the roots of the word actually mean "right praise." The Wesleys sought to praise God with every aspect of their being; head and heart and hands all worked together to praise the God of love. Perhaps this is why the singing of hymns was so important to them both. Singing involves the whole of who we are. They viewed life as a song to be sung to the praise of God in gratitude for all that God has done.

Spirituality. By spirituality here I simply mean a disciplined devotional life. Virtually every day of the Wesleys' lives began and ended with the recitation of Morning Prayer and Evening Prayer out of the Book of Common Prayer. Prayer framed each day, and not just any prayer, but some of the most important prayers of Christian devotion, such as the Magnificat, Mary's song of praise from Luke; the Te Deum ("Thee, O God, we praise"), an early Christian hymn; and the great Collects, or prayers of Thomas Cranmer, the author of the Book of Common Prayer. The classic spiritual disciplines, from Bible study and Eucharist to helping the poor and waging peace, shaped their lives. They hand on this holistic spirituality to all who would embrace it today.

Mission. One of the most crucial insights that John and Charles carried with them throughout their lives was that the gospel—the good news of God's love revealed in Jesus—is a message for everyone. They understood themselves to be God's partners in a mission of love and service to others. One of Charles's most famous hymns, "O for a thousand tongues to sing," is nothing other than a mission manifesto:

My gracious Master and my God,
  Assist me to proclaim,
To spread through all the earth abroad
  The honors of thy name.

Order. Is it any wonder that the movement initiated by the Wesleys should come to be known as "Method-ism?" It is in large measure due to John's organizational genius that the evangelical revival developed into such a powerful religious awakening in his own day. But for the Wesleys, more than anything else, the disciplined ordering of life made it possible for them to find God present in all the activities of their days. They lived as those who, as the great Carmelite devotional writer, Brother Lawrence, wrote years before, practiced the presence of God in an intentional and disciplined way.

Scripture. John Wesley once described himself as a man of one book. The Wesleyan revival was, for all intents and purposes, a rediscovery of the Bible. It was to Holy Scripture that John and Charles returned time and time again for inspiration, for focus, for life. They had an insatiable appetite for God's Word, and that Word shaped virtually everything they did. They helped others discover that this book was not simply "dead words" from long ago but God's "Living Word" to us today.

John and Charles Wesley viewed life as a way of devotion. This metaphor offers, perhaps, the best approach to this book. All people, Christian or otherwise, are involved in a journey throughout the course of their lives. They seek to understand who they are and what their place is in this world. These brothers point to a spiritual path that all people can benefit from regardless of their religious heritage or perspective. The excerpts from the writings of the Wesleys that follow provide an introduction to a theology and spirituality that has much to offer to those who seek God today. Perhaps this is the first step in a pilgrimage leading to profound insights and commitments that will shape the rest of your life. If so, the Wesleys would be pleased indeed. Hopefully, you will understand the Wesleys better and seek to know more about their amazing legacy through your encounter with them here. The best possible scenario would be, if, like Charles, you find yourself "lost in wonder, love, and praise" in the contemplation of the God of grace through their witness.

PART ONE

Autobiographical Portraits

A Preacher of Grace and a Poet of Love

✠ The quest for holiness characterized the life of John Wesley from beginning to end. Transformation stood at the center of his vision of the Christian life and was an essential component of the lifelong journey leading to holiness of heart and life. He saw conversion as an illuminating paradigm of how God's grace functions in the life of the believer. He viewed the Christian life as a way of salvation, in which people experience God's offer of relationship and restoration in terms of personal transformation. In *A Plain Account of Christian Perfection* (1766), Wesley's magnum opus, he explains this vision of discipleship and its goal of perfect love. He drew his conception of total dedication to God from multiple sources.

1 As a young student at Oxford University, the writings of Bishop Jeremy Taylor (1613–1667) impressed Wesley deeply. Taylor's twin volumes, *The Rule and Exercise of Holy Living* (1650) and *The Rule and Exercise of Holy Dying* (1651), left an indelible mark. Both handbooks emphasized the importance of purity with regard to motivation or intention.

2 Many scholars describe this resolution as Wesley's "religious conversion." Standing on the threshold of his ordination as a deacon in the Church of England, he determines to commit the entirety of his life to God without reservation.

3 The devotional classic by the late medieval monk Thomas à Kempis is better known to many by its original title, *The Imitation of Christ*. The practical mysticism it teaches focuses on the centrality of the heart and the fullest possible conversion of the heart to God.

4 These two early works of William Law (1686–1761), *A Practical Treatise upon Christian Perfection* (1726) and *A Serious Call to a Devout and Holy Life* (1728), exerted tremendous influence on many devout Anglicans in the eighteenth century and beyond. Owing in large measure to the latter work, Wesley would never abandon his ideal of being an "altogether" rather than an "almost Christian."

☐ John Wesley

Conversion to God

In the year 1725, being in the twenty-third year of my age, I met with Bishop Taylor's *Rules and Exercises of Holy Living and Dying*.[1] In reading several parts of this book I was exceedingly affected; that part in particular which relates to purity of intention. Instantly I resolved to dedicate all my life to God, all my thoughts and words and actions, being thoroughly convinced there was no medium, but that every part of my life (not some only) must either be a sacrifice to God or myself, that is in effect, to the devil.[2]

Can any serious person doubt this or find a medium between serving God and serving the devil?

In the year 1726 I met with Kempis's *Christian's Pattern*.[3] The nature and extent of inward religion, the religion of the heart, now appeared to me in a stronger light than ever it had done before. I saw that giving even all my life to God (supposing it possible to do this and go no farther) would profit me nothing unless I gave my heart, yea all my heart, to God. I saw that "simplicity of intention, and purity of affection," one design in all we speak or do, and one desire ruling all our dispositions are indeed "the wings of the soul," without which she can never ascend to the mount of God.

A year or two after, Mr. Law's *Christian Perfection* and *Serious Call* were put into my hands.[4] These convinced me more than ever of the absolute impossibility of being half a Christian. And I determined, through God's grace (the absolute necessity of which I was deeply sensible of), to be all-devoted to God—to give God all my soul, my body, and my substance.

JW *A Plain Account of Christian Perfection* (1766),
2–4 (*Christian Perfection*, 5–6)

⊹ Undoubtedly containing the most remembered words of John Wesley, this excerpt from his published journal describes the so-called Aldersgate Experience in which his heart was strangely warmed. Yet another critical turning point in his life, often described as his "evangelical conversion," this experience signals a monumental shift in Wesley's pilgrimage of faith. Over the course of the year 1738, Wesley became convinced that he did not need to become holy in order to earn God's forgiveness and love; rather, he came to believe that God already loved him just as he was and that holiness would spring naturally, then, out of that realization. To use more precise theological language, whereas prior to this turning point in his life Wesley believed that sanctification preceded justification, as a consequence of this experience, he understood that justification provides the foundation upon which a holy life (sanctification) can be built. The experience of God's overwhelming and unconditional love, which he describes using the language of assurance, reoriented his thinking and his life in radical ways. No longer driven to prove his acceptability to God, he experienced the liberating power of God's grace.

One of the most important things to note is Wesley's use of personal pronouns in this account: "an assurance was given me that he had taken away *my* sins, even *mine*, and saved *me* from the law of sin and death." In every subsequent printing of his journal, he italicized these words. These personal pronouns reflect what Robert Cushman, a former dean of Duke Divinity School, once described as the "enpersonalization of faith." The personal relationship that God seeks to establish with all people is one of the most critical issues for every human being in his or her spiritual journey. It is not too much to say that the objective faith *in which* Wesley believed, up to this point, became the subjective faith *by which* he believed. This living faith fueled the movement of renewal he led.

5 The term "society" simply means a small group of devout Christians seeking to help one another in their journey of faith.

A Heartwarming Experience of Grace

I think it was about five this morning that I opened my Testament on those words ... "There are given unto us exceeding great and precious promises, even that ye should be partakers of the divine nature." Just as I went out I opened it again on those words, "Thou art not far from the kingdom of God." In the afternoon I was asked to go to St. Paul's. The anthem was, "Out of the deep have I called unto thee, O Lord. Lord, hear my voice."

In the evening I went very unwillingly to a society in Aldersgate Street[5] where one was reading Luther's Preface to the Epistle to the Romans. About a quarter before nine, while he was describing the change which God works in the heart through faith in Christ, I felt my heart strangely warmed. I felt I did trust in Christ, Christ alone for salvation, and an assurance was given me that he had taken away *my* sins, even *mine*, and saved *me* from the law of sin and death.

I began to pray with all my might for those who had in a more especial manner despitefully used me and persecuted me. I then testified openly to all there what I now first felt in my heart. But it was not long before the enemy suggested, "This cannot be faith, for where is your joy?" Then was I taught that *peace and victory over sin are essential to faith in the Captain of our salvation, but that as to the transports of joy* that usually attend the beginning of it, especially in those who have mourned deeply, *God sometimes gives, sometimes withholds them, according to the counsels of God's own will.*

After my return home I was much buffeted with temptations but cried out and they fled away. They returned again and again. I as often lifted up my eyes, and he "sent me help from his holy place." And herein I found the difference between this and my former state chiefly consisted. I was striving, yea fighting with all my might under the law, as well as under grace. But then I was sometimes, if not often, conquered; now, I was always conqueror.

JW *Journal*, May 24, 1738, 13–16 (*Works*, 18:249–50)

☩ The singing of hymns by a group of German Pietists known as Moravians had deeply impressed Wesley during the lengthy and treacherous sea journey to the colony of Georgia in 1735. In order to talk with these new friends and to learn more about their faith, he determined to learn the German language. He later translated many of these hymns into English, and his rendering of this hymn of Johann Scheffler (1624–1677) is, perhaps, one of Wesley's best translations. In this lyrical work of art, the salient characteristics of Wesley's own life— total commitment to God, the centrality of love, the quest for holiness, gratitude to God—coalesce in a powerful expression of Christian devotion.

Gratitude to God

Thee will I love, my strength, my tower,
 Thee will I love, my joy, my crown,
Thee will I love with all my power,
 In all my works, and thee alone;
Thee will I love, till the pure fire
Fill my whole soul with chaste desire.

Give to mine eyes refreshing tears,
 Give to my heart chaste, hallowed fires,
Give to my soul, with filial fears,
 The love that all heaven's host inspires;
That all my powers, with all their might,
In thy sole glory may unite.

Thee will I love, my joy, my crown,
 Thee will I love, my Lord, my God,
Thee will I love beneath thy frown
 Or smile, thy scepter or thy rod;
What though my flesh and heart decay?
Thee shall I love in endless day!

> JW TRANS., JOHANN SCHEFFLER HYMN, "ICH WILL DICH LIEBEN, MEINE STÄRKE"
> (*HYMNS AND SACRED POEMS* [*HSP*] [1739], 198–200, STANZAS 1, 6–7)

6 As a scrupulous priest of the Church of England, Wesley had prided himself on his adherence to the regulations of his church. In the eighteenth century, a priest was only permitted to preach in a building dedicated for that purpose and, if outside his own parish, only with the permission of the priest in charge or the bishop. George Whitefield (1714–1770), a fellow priest and friend from his Oxford days, had begun the practice of preaching out-of-doors to the poor in the area surrounding Bristol. Having begun this work, but now ready to embark for America, Whitefield sought Wesley's assistance in this irregular ministry.

7 April 2, 1739, marks the birth of Methodism as a movement of renewal within the Church of England. Following his experience at Aldersgate, Wesley proclaimed his newfound faith, only to receive a rather dusty welcome from dubious colleagues in ministry or straightforward prohibitions from those who considered him to be an "enthusiast"—what we would call a religious fanatic today. His radical message of spiritual liberation and the equality of all people before God proved to be too revolutionary, particularly to those in power who preferred the status quo. But Wesley was convinced beyond any doubt that God intended the message of love and grace in Christ for all people. Once he broke through his own scruples and began to preach to the poor in the fields, the response overwhelmed him. It is not too much to say that his actions birthed a movement, and he began to devote his energies to the spiritual care of those who were awakened by his preaching. Instead of waiting for people to come to him, he went out to the people wherever they could be found.

The Birth of Methodism

In the evening [March 31] I reached Bristol and met Mr. Whitefield there. I could scarce reconcile myself at first to this *strange way* of preaching in the fields, of which he set me an example on Sunday, having been all my life (till very lately) so tenacious of every point relating to decency and order that I should have thought the *saving* of souls *almost a sin* if it had not been done *in a church*.**6**

April 1. In the evening (Mr. Whitefield being gone) I began expounding our Lord's Sermon on the Mount (one pretty remarkable precedent of *field preaching*, though I suppose *there were churches* at that time also) to a little society which was accustomed to meet once or twice a week in Nicholas Street.

Mon. 2. At four in the afternoon I submitted to "be more vile," and proclaimed in the highways the glad tidings of salvation, speaking from a hillside adjoining to the city to about three hundred people. The scripture on which I spoke was this (is it possible anyone should be ignorant that it is fulfilled in every true minister of Christ?): "The Spirit of the Lord is upon me because he hath anointed me to preach the gospel to the poor. He hath sent me to heal the broken-hearted, to preach deliverance to the captives and recovery of sight to the blind, to set at liberty them that are bruised, to proclaim the acceptable year of the Lord."**7**

JW *JOURNAL*, MARCH 31, APRIL 2, 1739 (*WORKS*, 19:46)

8 Even some of John Wesley's friends criticized his actions. In a letter, most likely to a former member of the so-called Holy Club at Oxford—a group of devout young men who sought to live out their life of faith in a disciplined pattern of personal piety and social service—he provides one of his earliest apologies, or defenses, of his work. In his response to criticism, Wesley alludes frequently to scripture, building a defense of his actions, not only upon his own, reasoned arguments but also upon God's Word.

9 John Wesley had served as a parish priest under his father's direction for a brief period of time. But, as a fellow of Lincoln College at Oxford, he did not have a congregation of his own. All of life, at that time, revolved around the "parish," since the church was the center of community life. One of his most famous statements—"I look upon all *the world as my parish"*—reflects Wesley's expansive vision and sets the tone for the mission of his movement. His hope is nothing less than to spread scriptural holiness throughout the whole land.

A World Parish

I allow no other rule, whether of faith or practice, than the Holy Scriptures.[8] But on scriptural principles I do not think it hard to justify whatever I do. God in scripture commands me, according to my power, to instruct the ignorant, reform the wicked, confirm the virtuous. Man forbids me to do this in another's parish, that is, in effect, to do it at all, seeing I have now no parish of my own nor probably ever shall. Whom then shall I hear? God or man? "If it be just to obey man rather than God, judge you." "A dispensation of the gospel is committed to me, and woe is me if I preach not the gospel." But where shall I preach it upon the principles you mention? Why, not in Europe, Asia, Africa, or America; not in any of the Christian parts, at least, of the habitable earth. For all these are, after a sort, divided into parishes. If it be said, "Go back then to the heathens from whence you came," nay, but neither could I now (on your principles) preach to them, for all the heathens in Georgia belong to the parish either of Savannah or Frederica.

Suffer me now to tell you *my* principles in this matter. I look upon all *the world as my parish*. Thus far I mean that, in whatever part of it I am, I judge it meet, right, and my bounden duty to declare unto all that are willing to hear the glad tidings of salvation.[9] This is the work which I know God has called me to. And I am sure that God's blessing attends it. Great encouragement have I therefore to be faithful in fulfilling the work God has given me to do. I am God's servant and as such am employed (glory be to God) day and night in God's service. I am employed according to the plain direction of God's Word, "As I have opportunity, doing good unto all men." And his providence clearly concurs with his Word, which has disengaged me from all things else that I might singly attend on this very thing "and go about doing good."

JW LETTER TO JOHN CLAYTON, MARCH 28, 1739 (*WORKS*, 25:615–16)

10 John Wesley was a consummate communicator. Nothing was more important to him than proclaiming the good news of God's love in as clear and understandable a manner as possible. Preaching was his primary medium. Over the course of his life he preached literally thousands of sermons, and all of those in widely different contexts. Many of the sermons, including those in his multivolume *Sermons on Several Occasions* from which this excerpt is taken, he never actually preached. These prose sermons might be more properly described as sermonic essays—topical sermons in which he presented the essence of his thinking with regard to primary Christian teaching—essays meant more to be read than heard. In order to get a sense of what Wesley's actual preaching was like, it is necessary to consult contemporary eyewitness accounts. In these accounts, one word stands out above all others: "now." Urgency characterized his actual extemporaneous preaching, and 2 Corinthians 6:2 captures the thrust of his message: "Now is the day of salvation." His primary goal was to communicate the truth of the gospel in a way that connected directly and persuasively with the real people to whom he preached.

Plain Words for Plain People

I design plain truth for plain people.[10] Therefore of set purpose I abstain from all nice and philosophical speculations, from all perplexed and intricate reasoning, and as far as possible from even the show of learning, unless in sometimes citing the original scriptures. I labor to avoid all words which are not easy to be understood, all which are not used in common life, and, in particular, those kinds of technical terms that so frequently occur in bodies of divinity, those modes of speaking which men of reading are intimately acquainted with, but which to common people are an unknown tongue. Yet I am not assured that I do not sometimes slide into them unawares. It is so extremely natural to imagine that a word which is familiar to ourselves is so to all the world. Nay, my design is, in some sense, to forget all that ever I have read in my life. I mean to speak, in general, as if I had never read one author, ancient or modern (always excepting the inspired). I am persuaded that ... this may be a means of enabling me more clearly to express the sentiments of my heart, while I simply follow the chain of my own thoughts, without entangling myself with those of other people.

JW *Sermons on Several Occasions*, Preface, I.3–4 (*Works*, 1:104)

11 Throughout the course of his life, Wesley spent a lot of time among the poor. While his Oxford training and professional credentials placed him in a class above many with whom he associated, he had experienced the realities of poverty early in life. Even his father, Samuel, spent time in a debtor's prison, rescued only by the generosity of his bishop. Poverty was endemic in Wesley's day, and the early years of the industrial revolution witnessed major demographic shifts that exacerbated many of the social problems associated with deprivation. People flocked to the burgeoning cities in search of work, abandoning the agrarian style of life they had known for generations. But often, there was no work to be found. Wesley was committed to the poor, and experiences like the one upon which he reflects here deepened his resolve to connect the Christian faith with the pressing needs of people in his time. He sought to live in solidarity, as much as he could, with the least and last of society; he never separated physical from spiritual needs. He urged others to avoid extravagance in clothes and home furnishings so as to be more generous, instead, to needy neighbors (see Matthew 25:31–46).

Concern for the Poor

Many years ago when I was at Oxford, on a cold winter's day a young maid ... called upon me. I said: "You seem half starved. Have you nothing to cover you but that thin linen gown?" She said, "Sir, this is all I have!" I put my hand in my pocket, but found I had scarce any money left, having just paid away what I had. It immediately struck me, will not your Master say, "'Well done, good and faithful steward?' Thou hast adorned thy walls with the money which might have screened this poor creature from the cold!" O justice! O mercy! Are not these pictures the blood of this poor maid! See your expensive apparel in the same light— your gown, hat, headdress! Everything about you which cost more than Christian duty required you to lay out is the blood of the poor! O be wise for the time to come! Be more merciful! More faithful to God and neighbor! More abundantly "adorned (like men and women professing godliness) with good works!"[11]

JW SERMON "ON DRESS" (1786), 16 (*WORKS*, 3:255)

12 The Wesleys believed that God created human beings in God's own image. They also believed, however, that sin defaced this image. As we will see later, salvation has to do with the recovery of this image in our lives. Since love, more than anything else, characterizes God's nature, the recovery of God's image entails our becoming the loving creatures God intends us to be.

13 John Wesley was not a systematic theologian. Much like Augustine, his theology was hammered out on the crucible of controversy and in dialogue with both his opponents and his friends. In this letter to a friend from his Oxford days, he provides one of his best definitions of "religion." This correspondence predated his Aldersgate Experience, but note the consistency with regard to his fundamental conception in the subsequent statements. True religion stands at the very core of our being and is linked to words like *renewal, recovery*, and *conformity*, all of which have to do with our reason for being in love. Some of their contemporaries thought the Wesleys were religious fanatics or extremists; the term they used was "enthusiasts." If enthusiasts at all, a label the Wesleys always rejected, they were "reasonable enthusiasts."

14 This phrase simply means at peace in their hearts.

15 The term "new covenant" refers to the new relationship between God and humans mediated by Jesus Christ, which is open to all people.

16 In one of Wesley's most important defenses of Methodism, *An Earnest Appeal to Men of Reason and Religion* (1743), he recalls a conversation he shared with a young man who had attempted suicide. Wesley, engaging in dialogue here with someone who was genuinely seeking to find purpose and meaning in life, reveals the compassion and urgency that characterized his vision of real religion. True religion—the religion of love—always produces happiness and joy.

A Definition of Religion

I take religion to be, not the bare saying over so many prayers morning and evening, in public or in private—not anything superadded now and then to a careless or worldly life—but a constant ruling habit of soul, a renewal of our minds in the image of God, a recovery of the divine likeness,[12] an increasing conformity of heart and life to the pattern of our most holy Redeemer. But if this is religion, if this is that way to life which our blessed Lord has marked out for us, how can any, while they keep close to this way, be charged with running into extremes?[13]

JW LETTER TO RICHARD MORGAN, JANUARY 15, 1734 (*WORKS*, 25:369)

"What religion do you preach? What is it good for?" I replied, "I *do* preach to as many as desire to hear, every night and morning." You ask what I would do with them. I would make them virtuous and happy, easy in themselves[14] and useful to others. Where would I lead them? To heaven—to God the Judge, the lover of all, and to Jesus the Mediator of the new covenant.[15] What religion do I preach? The religion of love—the law of kindness brought to light by the gospel. What is this good for? To make all who receive it enjoy God and themselves, to make them, like God, lovers of all, contented in their lives and crying out at their death in calm assurance, "O grave, where is thy victory?... Thanks be unto God, who giveth *me* the victory, through *my* Lord Jesus Christ."[16]

JW *AN EARNEST APPEAL TO MEN OF REASON AND RELIGION* (1743), 19 (*WORKS*, 11:51)

17 Gratitude and benevolence are the keynotes of Wesley's conception of genuine Christianity. Gratitude is the response of the creature to the Creator; the response of those who are reconciled to the Reconciler. God's reconciling love produces grateful hearts and lives characterized by thanksgiving. Second, benevolence or good will is the response of the disciple whose vision of life has been transformed by the God of love. Having discovered God's purpose for life and their place within God's unfolding story, disciples of Jesus immerse themselves in and commit themselves to God's vision for a just and peace-filled world.

18 Albert Outler once described Wesley as a eudaemonist. That is a fancy word that means his whole conception of life was oriented toward happiness; perhaps a better word would be "blessedness" in the sense that it is used in the Beatitudes. Wesley's main concern in life was human happiness. The genuine follower of Jesus is a happy person whose life is characterized by joy, mercy, kindness, and justice. Radical trust in the sufficiency of God's grace leads to love, of both God and neighbor, and to a quality of happiness in life that can only be attributed to the indwelling of the Spirit in the life of the believer.

True religion is right dispositions towards God and neighbor. It is, in two words, gratitude and benevolence—gratitude to our Creator and supreme Benefactor and benevolence to our fellow creatures.[17] In other words, it is the loving God with all our heart and our neighbor as ourselves.

It is in consequence of our knowing God loves us that we love God and love our neighbor as ourselves. Gratitude toward our Creator cannot but produce benevolence to our fellow creatures. The love of Christ constrains us, not only to be harmless—to do no ill to our neighbor—but to be useful, to be "zealous of good works," "as we have time to do good unto all" and be patterns to all of true genuine morality, of justice, mercy, and truth. This is religion and this is happiness, the happiness for which we were made.[18] This begins when we begin to know God by the teaching of God's own Spirit. As soon as the Father of spirits reveals the Son in our hearts and the Son reveals his Father, the love of God is shed abroad in our hearts. Then, and not till then, are we happy. We are happy, first, in the consciousness of God's favor, which indeed is better than life itself. Next, in the constant communion with the Father, and with the Son, Jesus Christ. Then in all the heavenly dispositions which God has wrought in us by the Spirit. Again, in the testimony of the Spirit that all our works please God. And, lastly, in the testimony of our own spirit that "in simplicity and godly sincerity we have had our conversation in the world." Standing fast in this liberty from sin and sorrow, wherewith Christ has made them free, real Christians "rejoice evermore, pray without ceasing, and in everything give thanks." And their happiness still increases as they "grow up into the measure of the stature of the fullness of Christ."

JW SERMON "THE UNITY OF THE DIVINE BEING" (1789), 16–17 (*WORKS*, 4:66–67)

19 In Susanna, the mother of the Wesleys, there was a strong underlying sentiment expressed tersely in the phrase "deeds, not creeds." While not dismissive of Christian doctrine, she had nurtured a healthy distrust of rigid statements, reflecting a nondogmatic strain that typified much of the Anglican tradition. John followed suit. Moreover, he was convinced that most of the bloodshed in previous generations originated in religious conflicts over "opinions" and not over matters of essential Christian doctrine. His 1750 sermon "Catholic Spirit" articulated this viewpoint, advocating unity in essentials and charity with regard to opinions. The term "catholic" here means "universal." It does not refer to Roman Catholicism. This spirit ran widely throughout his theological corpus and was reflected by the manner in which he debated other Christian believers. He exhibited a wide embrace and was content "to think and let think" on many issues that, in contradistinction, led others to despise and vilify their Christian brothers and sisters. While sounding soft-headed to some, perhaps, he was convinced that love was the surest avenue to truth.

20 To "fear God" here means to stand in awe of God, to honor and glorify God properly.

21 For the Christian, God rules in the hearts and lives of people now; that is the present Kingdom. The eternal Kingdom refers to everlasting life with Jesus in heaven.

22 The unbelieving world often has its unbelief confirmed by witnessing the way in which Christians deal with one another in controversy. Philipp Jakob Spener (1635–1705), the founder of German Pietism, made this point explicitly in his classic work, *Pia Desideria* (*Heartfelt Desire*). While Christians might disagree substantively on some issues, he argued, they should make certain that love and a genuine concern to understand their opponents govern the manner in which they debate. Despite the fact that Wesley sometimes failed to live up to this noble vision, he kept his eye firmly fixed on this lofty ideal.

A Spirit of Toleration

If then we take this word in the strictest sense, persons of a catholic spirit are those who, in the manner mentioned above, give their hand to all whose hearts are right with their hearts.[19] They know how to value and praise God for all the advantages they enjoy, with regard to the knowledge of the things of God, the true, scriptural manner of worshiping God, and above all, their union with a congregation fearing God[20] and working righteousness. They retain these blessings with the strictest care, keeping them as the apple of their eye. They love one another as friends, as companions in the Lord, as members of Christ and children of God, as joint partakers now of the present kingdom of God, and fellow-heirs of God's eternal Kingdom.[21] All of whatever opinion or worship or congregation who believe in the Lord Jesus Christ, who love God and neighbor, who rejoice to please and fear to offend God, are careful to abstain from evil and zealous of good works. Those disciples are of a truly catholic spirit who bear all these continually upon their hearts, who, having an unspeakable tenderness for their persons and longing for their welfare, do not cease to commend them to God in prayer, as well as to plead their cause before others. They speak comfortingly to them and labor by all their words to strengthen their hands in God.[22] They assist them to the uttermost of their power in all things, spiritual and temporal. They are ready "to spend and be spent for them," even to lay down their lives for their sake.

JW SERMON "CATHOLIC SPIRIT" (1750), III.5 (*WORKS*, 2:94–95)

✙ Despite the fact that Charles was the younger of the two brothers, it is interesting how the hymn writer often led the way in the matter of "firsts." Charles, in fact, started the small group movement at Oxford University later described as the Holy Club—the first rise of Methodism. John came after this fellowship had been established and immediately assumed its leadership. With regard to the birth of Methodism in the field preaching among the Kingswood miners, it must be remembered that Charles launched into these activities a few days before his brother had even arrived on the scene. Here, in an excerpt from Charles Wesley's journal, we discover that his "evangelical conversion"—placing one's trust and confidence in Jesus Christ as savior and experiencing the assurance of faith—preceded that of his brother by three days. Charles has often stood in the shadow of his older brother, but his influence upon John must never be forgotten.

1 He awaited the coming of God into his life.

2 Note the way in which scripture plays a central role in his narrative of the conversion. All these texts have to do with the way in which God finds a home in the human heart.

3 How amazing that one of the greatest hymn writers of all time found confirmation in these words.

4 Several critical aspects of Charles's own spiritual pilgrimage come into focus in this paragraph. These discoveries were part and parcel of his experience. First, faith restores one's relationship with God. No one can produce this kind of trust on the basis of his or her own efforts. Rather, the capacity to entrust one's life to God is one of God's greatest gifts. Second, a right relationship with God produces genuine peace and joy. Third, only the presence of Jesus can sustain us in this journey deeper into God's love.

☐ Charles Wesley

Evangelical Conversion

I woke in hope and expectation of Christ's coming.[1] At nine my brother and some friends came and sang a hymn to the Holy Ghost. My comfort and hope were hereby increased. In about half-an-hour they went. I engaged in prayer, the substance as follows: "O Jesus, thou hast said, 'I will come unto you;' thou hast said, 'I will send the Comforter unto you;' thou hast said, 'My Father and I will come unto you, and make our abode with you.' Thou art God who canst not lie. I wholly rely upon thy most true promise. Accomplish it in thy time and manner."[2] ....

I rose and looked into the scripture. The words that first presented were, "And now, Lord, what is my hope? Truly my hope is even in thee." I then cast down my eye and met, "He hath put a new song in my mouth, even a thanksgiving unto our God. Many shall see it, and fear, and shall put their trust in the Lord."[3] ....

I now found myself at peace with God and rejoiced in hope of loving Christ. My disposition for the rest of the day was mistrust of my own great, but before unknown, weakness. I saw that by faith I stood—by the continual support of faith—which kept me from falling, though of myself I am ever sinking into sin. I went to bed still sensible of my own weakness (I humbly hope to be more and more so), yet confident of Christ's protection.[4]

CW JOURNAL, MAY 21, 1738 (CW JOURNAL, 1:90–92)

(continued on page 51)

5 Like most great theologians, such as St. Augustine, Charles identifies pride as the root of all sin. The essence of pride is to put ourselves in the place of God. Charles seeks to avoid this at all costs.

6 Note how Charles's default mode is to articulate his experience in a lyrical form. This poetic tendency in all things defines his life. Poetry functions for him as the primary means by which to express all human experience. Not only can this lyrical expression lift the human spirit, but it can also express the agony and ecstasy of life and communicate the central teachings of the Christian faith. In Methodism, the hymns of Charles Wesley both express and teach the miracle of divine/human encounter and its meaning.

7 That is, the Sacrament of Holy Communion.

8 John flies almost immediately to Charles's side to share with his brother the good news of his own saving experience of God's grace. They celebrate their common joy by singing the praise of God, using the hymn, no doubt, that Charles had just composed.

I woke under the protection of Christ and gave myself up, soul and body, to him. At nine I began a hymn upon my conversion, but was persuaded to break off for fear of pride.[5] Mr. Bray, coming, encouraged me to proceed in spite of Satan. I prayed Christ to stand by me and finished the hymn.[6]

Wed., May 24th. Planning to receive the Sacrament today,[7] I was assaulted by the fear of my old accustomed deadness, but soon recovered my confidence in Christ, that he would give me so much sense of his love now as he saw good for me. I received without any sensible devotion, much as I used to be, only that I was afterwards perfectly calm and satisfied, without doubt, fear, or scruple.... At eight I prayed by myself for love, with some seeing and assurance of feeling more. Towards ten my brother was brought in triumph by a troop of our friends and declared, "I believe." We sang the hymn with great joy and parted with prayer.[8] At midnight I gave myself up to Christ, assured I was safe, sleeping or waking. Had continual experience of his power to overrule all temptation and confessed, with joy and surprise, that he was able to do exceedingly abundantly for me above what I can ask or think.

CW JOURNAL, MAY 23–24, 1738 (CW JOURNAL, 1:94–95)

✠ Scholars still debate whether this or some other hymn was the one composed by Charles to celebrate his conversion. Most believe, however, that this is the text to which he alludes in the journal. The title of this hymn, "Christ the Friend of Sinners," reflects the hymn writer's favorite title for Jesus. The language of God as friend, and Jesus as friend of sinners, in particular, pervades his hymns. This reveals a concept at the very heart of Wesleyan theology: God is for us, not against us. God reaches out to all with the offer of abiding friendship. God demonstrates this in a most unfathomable way—God enters into human history in the person of Jesus and into our own lives through the power of the Spirit.

9 The hymn opens with penetrating, even haunting questions that reflect the way Charles was overcome by awe and wonder. How is it possible, he ponders, that God could love us—love *me*—so much?

10 Charles alludes to the famous Epworth rectory fire of 1709 and the miraculous rescue of his brother John. Whereas Susanna used this language in reference to John and God's providential care of him in this catastrophe—calling him "a brand plucked from the burning"—Charles transforms the image into a metaphor of salvation for all who put their trust in Jesus.

11 Antepast here means a glimpse or foretaste of heaven.

12 This is Wesley's shorthand description of sinful humanity in need of a savior.

13 Here is the wide embrace of Wesleyan Christianity. Jesus opens his arms wide to all.

14 This stanza describes the spirit of Jesus. For Charles, hospitality represents the essence of the Christian faith. Through his sacrifice, Jesus demonstrates how God seeks to "make you room," "take you in," "invite you home." We partner in God's mission in the world as we imitate this spirit of welcome and hospitality.

The Conversion Hymn

Where shall my wondering soul begin?
  How shall I all to heaven aspire?[9]
A slave redeemed from death and sin,
  A brand plucked from eternal fire,[10]
How shall I equal triumphs raise,
Or sing my great deliverer's praise?

O how shall I the goodness tell,
  Father, which thou to me hast showed?
That I, a child of wrath and hell,
  I should be called a child of God!
Should know, should feel my sins forgiven,
Blessed with this antepast[11] of heaven!

Outcasts of men, to you I call,
  Harlots and publicans and thieves;[12]
He spreads his arms to embrace you all,[13]
  Sinners alone his grace receive.
No need of him the righteous have;
He came the lost to seek and save!

Come, O my guilty brethren, come,
  Groaning beneath your load of sin;
His bleeding heart shall make you room,
  His open side shall take you in.
He calls you now, invites you home—
Come, O my guilty brethren, come![14]

CW HYMN "CHRIST THE FRIEND OF SINNERS"
(*HSP* [1739], 101–3, STANZAS 1–2, 5, 7)

✝ Though this is one of the most widely sung hymns of Charles Wesley, most people do not realize the mission orientation of the text. It was composed of eighteen stanzas in its original form, and the first third of the hymn recounts Charles's conversion experience. The title of the hymn reveals the fact that he composed this lyrical offering of praise on the anniversary of his conversion. The opening line of stanza seven, one of the most famous statements in his verse, may reflect the comment of the Wesleys' Moravian friend and spiritual guide, Peter Böhler, who said on one occasion that if he had a thousand tongues, he would use them all to praise God. In these familiar stanzas, Charles expands his appeal to praise God to everyone everywhere. In the hymn, as in life, praise of God moves seamlessly into mission in the world.

15 Charles reinforces the understanding that God is a God of action. Through Jesus, God breaks down barriers, liberates, cleans, speaks, resurrects, heals. In this and the subsequent stanza, he articulates a threefold meaning of salvation. Jesus' redemptive work liberates us from the punishment, guilt, and power of sin in our lives. New life begins in putting our trust in this liberating God.

Discipleship in Mission

O for a thousand tongues to sing
  My dear Redeemer's praise!
The glories of my God and King,
  The triumphs of his grace.

My gracious Master and my God,
  Assist me to proclaim,
To spread through all the earth abroad
  The honors of thy name.

Jesus! the name that charms our fears,
  That bids our sorrows cease;
'Tis music in the sinner's ears,
  'Tis life, and health, and peace!

He breaks the power of canceled sin,
  He sets the prisoner free;
His blood can make the foulest clean;
  His blood availed for me.[15]

He speaks, and listening to his voice,
  New life the dead receive;
The mournful, broken hearts rejoice,
  The humble poor *believe*.

Hear him, ye deaf; his praise, ye dumb,
  Your loosened tongues employ;
Ye blind, behold your Savior come,
  And leap, ye lame, for joy.

CW HYMN "FOR THE ANNIVERSARY DAY OF ONE'S CONVERSION"
(*HSP* [1740], 120–22, STANZAS 7–12)

16 Smallpox devastated families and communities in the eighteenth century. In this hymn, "For a Child in the Small-pox," Charles pours out his heart to God in prayer on behalf of his son. No hymn expresses human pathos more profoundly than this one. Charles, unlike his older brother, enjoyed an idyllic marriage and the joys and agonies of parenthood. Like most families of that time, he and Sally grieved the loss of children to death, and this experience in life deepened Charles's capacity for compassion. The child of whom he sings here, a musical prodigy by all accounts, did not survive this ordeal.

17 In the two concluding stanzas of the hymn, Charles plumbs the depths of the mystery of human suffering. Rather than providing an answer to the question of theodicy—the attempt to understand and explain God's goodness in the face of evil—Charles points to a God who stands alongside us and suffers with us in life. Because God sojourned among us in this broken world in the person of Jesus, God knows what suffering means to us. The images that Charles creates in these lines are staggering. Jesus weeps with us in our sorrow. Jesus blends our tears with his own. The hymn concludes, not with a stoic resignation to the pain and agony of life, but with an affirmation that the One who has stood with us will never abandon us and loves every person with an undying love. This hymn reveals as much to us about Charles as it does about his vision of God. Here was a man who knew life—a man who loved deeply and soared triumphantly.

Pathos in Life

Life and death are in thine hand;
   In thine hand our child we see
Waiting thy benign command,
   Less beloved by us than thee.[16]
Need we then his life request?
   Jesus understands our fears,
Reads a mother's panting breast,
   Knows the meaning of her tears.

Human tears may freely flow
   Authorized by tears divine,
'Till thine awful will we know,
   Comprehend thy whole design.
Jesus wept! And so may we;
   Jesus suffering all thy will,
Felt the soft infirmity,
   Feels his creature's sorrow still.[17]

Jesus blends them with his own,
   Mindful of his suffering days.
Father, hear thy pleading Son,
   Son of man for us he prays.
What for us he asks, bestow;
   Ours he makes his own request;
Send us life or death, we know,
   Life or death from thee is best.

CW HYMN "FOR A CHILD IN THE SMALL-POX"
(FAMILY HYMNS [1767], 76–78, STANZAS 4, 6–7)

18 Humility is the key to the Christian life. Charles learned this lesson early, through the example of his parents, the witness of great devotional writers like Thomas à Kempis, and primarily the life of Jesus. One of the earliest hymns of the church, recorded by St. Paul in Philippians 2:5–11, functioned as a paradigm of authentic life for Charles. It speaks of Jesus as the One who did not think of equality with God as something to be grasped; rather, he humbled himself and became the servant of all. The image of Jesus washing the feet of his disciples became another image that Charles frequently linked to authentic discipleship. The true disciple of Jesus is the humble child of God who serves.

19 Charles frequently uses the image of "the single eye" to indicate our need to focus on Jesus in all things. He set his aim on the glory of God in everything he did. St. Irenaeus, the second-century bishop and theologian of Lyons, believed that the greatest glory of God is the human being fully alive and that nothing brings a human being fully to life more than the effort to bring glory to God. This is how Charles lived.

20 Many of the great theologians of the early church summarized their teaching about salvation in this simple phrase: Jesus became what we are in order that we might become what he is. This stanza reflects that same vision and combines elements of Romans 12 and Ephesians 3 to create a powerful montage of consecration. Charles prays for God to fill the consecrated heart and to transform the captivated mind so that the disciple might be filled with all the fullness of God.

A Consecrated Heart

God of almighty love,
By whose sufficient grace
I lift my heart to things above,
And humbly seek thy face;
Through Jesus Christ the just
My faint desires receive,
And let me in thy goodness trust,
And to thy glory live.[18]

Whate'er I speak, or do,
Thy glory be my aim;
My offerings all are offered through
The ever-blessed name.
Jesus, my single eye
Is fixed on thee alone,
Thy name be praised on earth, on high,
Thy will by all be done.[19]

Spirit of grace, inspire
My consecrated heart,
Fill me with pure, celestial fire,
With all thou hast, or art.
My feeble mind transform,
And perfectly renewed
Into a saint exalt a worm,
A worm into a god![20]

CW HYMN "AN HOURLY ACT OF OBLATION"
(*HSP* [1749], 1:251–52, HYMN 37)

[✠] Music filled the house of Charles and Sally Wesley. It should be no surprise that Charles used music as an analogy for the Divine. In the world of music, Charles discovered untold insights about who God is and how God seeks to relate to all creation. This hymn of Methodism's "sweet singer" explores all these images and connections, the tones and harmonies of God.

[21] On one level, we come to know who we are most fully when we find our place in the greater harmony of God that surrounds us in life. To use an image drawn from C. S. Lewis's *The Chronicles of Narnia*, through Aslan—Lewis's figure of Jesus in the novels—God sang everything into existence. This actually reflects a more accurate translation of the Genesis account of creation. Charles encourages us to find our voice in God's great song of life.

[22] Charles contrasts the song of creation, as it were, with the new song of redemption in Jesus. Both songs are rooted in the keynote of grace. God's creation of all things out of nothing was a first great act of grace. Sin brought discord to this song, new tones and rhythms that disrupt and destroy the beauty that God intended. Redemption, then, restores the great song of life. It is not so much that redemption stands over against creation; rather, Jesus sings the song in a way that all can hear and respond; he restores the melody and harmony of the original creation. The new song of grace engages the whole person—potentially all people—in one great act of praise.

[23] Music functions as Charles's primary image here for heaven. The Shona of Zimbabwe, the dominant ethnic group of that nation, say that if you can talk you can sing; if you can walk you can dance. All heaven, Charles believes, sings and dances to the glory of God.

The Sweet Singer
Thou God of harmony and love,**21**
Whose name transports the saints above,
  And lulls the ravished spheres,
On thee in feeble strains I call,
And mix my humble voice with all
  The heavenly choristers.

Suffice for this the season past;
I come, great God, to learn at last
  The lesson of thy grace;
Teach me the new, the gospel song,**22**
And let my hand, my heart, my tongue
  Move only to thy praise.

Jesus! The heaven of heavens he is,
The soul of harmony and bliss!
  And while on him we gaze,
And while his glorious voice we hear,
Our spirits are all eye, all ear,
  And silence speaks his praise.

O might I die that awe to prove,
That prostrate awe which dares not move
  Before the great Three-One,
To shout by turns the bursting joy,
And all eternity employ
  In songs around the throne.**23**

CW HYMN "THE MUSICIAN'S HYMN" (*REDEMPTION HYMNS* [1747], 34–36,
HYMN 25, STANZAS 1, 4, 9–10)

⊹ Charles Wesley was fixated on love. The opening line of this hymn, "To love is all my wish," aptly describes his life and his singular aspiration. Wesley had a mystical bent that surfaces dramatically here. It is clear that he seeks to be swallowed up in God's love. All our loves find their beginning and ending in this great love that defines all life.

24 Charles provides a lyrical paraphrase of Ephesians 3:16–19: "I pray that, according to the riches of his glory, he may grant that you may be strengthened in your inner being with power through his Spirit, and that Christ may dwell in your hearts through faith, as you are being rooted and grounded in love. I pray that you may have the power to comprehend, with all the saints, what is the breadth and length and height and depth, and to know the love of Christ that surpasses knowledge, so that you may be filled with all the fullness of God."

25 Note Wesley's powerful use of verbs in this stanza. The soul swells to compass—to comprehend—God; it gasps, lives, and moves as it is filled, immersed, lost.

Lost in Love

To love is all my wish,
I only live for this:
Grant me, Lord, my heart's desire,
There by faith for ever dwell:
This I always will require
Thee and only thee to feel.

Thy power I pant to prove
Rooted and fixed in love,
Strengthened by thy Spirit's might,
Wise to fathom things divine,
What the length and breadth and height,
What the depth of love like thine.[24]

Ah! Give me this to know
With all thy saints below.
Swells my soul to compass thee,
Gasps in thee to live and move,
Filled with all the deity,
All immersed and lost in love![25]

CW HYMN "SAVIOR, THE WORLD'S AND MINE"
(*HSP* [1739], 168–69, STANZAS 4–6)

✠ Controversy always swirled around the Wesleys, in part because they simply did not conform to the religious norms of their day. They sought something more, something greater, something more profound than the ordinary. Being embroiled constantly in contentious situations, however, wearied them both. In this hymn that John appended to his sermon "Catholic Spirit," published as a separate pamphlet in 1755, Charles not only confesses this weariness, but more important, also portrays the wide embrace of the genuine Christian spirit.

26 Wesley embraced truth wherever he found it. Like one of the great early church apologists, Justin Martyr, he saw God's truth all around him. Regardless of the source, he was eager to make that truth his own, finding no discontinuity with the truth of Jesus. All truth connects inevitably with the One who is Truth.

27 These lines reveal an important principle that the Wesleys embraced fully: redemption through Jesus liberates, and liberation engenders a spirit of inclusivity, not exclusivity. The genuine Christian stands with open arms to embrace the world, not with a clenched fist to fight others.

28 This conception of the "hidden church" has a lengthy lineage. Some attribute the initial idea to St. Augustine; regardless, the Protestant reformers of the sixteenth century exploited the concept of a hidden or invisible church of God's faithful people as over against the visible institutional church as a human institution. The point is that Jesus unites the one true family of God, wherever it may be found, and the kindred spirit of fellowship that any experience is a wonderful gift from God.

A Wide Embrace

Weary of all this wordy strife,
　These notions, forms, and modes, and names,
To Thee, the Way, the Truth, the Life,
　Whose love my simple heart inflames,
Divinely taught, at last I fly,
With Thee and Thine to live and die.

Forth from the midst of Babel brought,
　Parties and sects I cast behind;
Enlarged my heart, and free my thought,
　Where'er the latent truth I find
The latent truth with joy to own,[26]
And bow to Jesus' name alone.

Redeemed by Thine almighty grace,
　I taste my glorious liberty,
With open arms the world embrace,
　But cleave to those who cleave to Thee;
But only in Thy saints delight,
Who walk with God in purest white.[27]

Joined to the hidden church unknown
　In this sure bond of perfectness;
Obscurely safe, I dwell alone
　And glory in the uniting grace,
To me, to each believer given,
To all Thy saints in earth and heaven.[28]

CW HYMN "CATHOLIC LOVE" (1755),
APPENDED TO JW SERMON "CATHOLIC SPIRIT"

⊹ Over the course of an extended illness during 1760–61, Charles put his confinement to good use in the production of a two-volume collection of lyrical reflections on many scriptural texts that arose from his reading of the entire Bible. While in much of his earlier work on the Psalms and other passages of the Bible he sought simply to paraphrase the original texts, this collection is much more reflective in tone. In his 1762 *Scripture Hymns*, he more often picks up a single theme, elaborates a particular image, or formulates a prayer provoked by his reading of the text.

In this two-stanza reflection on Leviticus 6:13: "A perpetual fire shall be kept burning on the altar; it shall not go out," he relates this image to the life of the individual Christian. Methodists later extended the same image to the movement of renewal that had become an inextinguishable blaze throughout Britain.

29 As the wise African American Quaker Howard Thurman once observed, the heart is the citadel of all our longings as human beings. We nurture our deepest dreams there and cling to our false ambitions as well. For Charles, the heart is the locus of the very presence of God—the Spirit of God—symbolized here by the flame.

30 Charles clarifies that this flame must be tended and nurtured with great care. He knew—intuitively, perhaps—that this great task could not be done alone. Only a community can sustain the flame of faith, keep it burning, and engender genuine, spiritual vitality. I have visited a number of monasteries in which an "eternal flame" is maintained by monks or nuns. This comes close to Wesley's vision. A community of friends, a succession of caregivers, and a fellowship of believers help each of us keep the flame burning.

An Inextinguishable Blaze

O thou who camest from above,
  The pure celestial fire to impart,
Kindle a flame of sacred love
  On the mean altar of my heart.[29]
There let it for thy glory burn
  With inextinguishable blaze,
And trembling to its source return,
  In humble prayer, and fervent praise.

Jesus, confirm my heart's desire
  To work and speak and think for thee;
Still let me guard the holy fire,[30]
  And still stir up thy gift in me.
Ready for all thy perfect will,
  My acts of faith and love repeat,
Till death thy endless mercies seal,
  And make my sacrifice complete.

CW HYMN ON LEVITICUS 6:13
(*SCRIPTURE HYMNS* [1762], 1:57, HYMN 183)

PART TWO

The Triune God of Grace and Love

1 In his sermon related to the doctrine of providence—God's sustaining and guiding care of the universe—John Wesley articulates an orthodox understanding of the view that God created all things out of nothing as a first great act of grace. God has no "need" for this universe or humanity within it, but it is the nature of love to reach out beyond itself, to overflow in the creation of new relationships of love. This also signals the relational nature of God, something expressed most powerfully in the doctrine of the Trinity. This doctrine affirms that God is a matrix of relationships—a dance of Father, Son, and Holy Spirit. Wesley's fourfold description of God as "eternal, almighty, all-wise, all-gracious" reflects the fundamental identity out of which Wesley believes all God's loving actions flow.

2 Wesley affirms the fundamental goodness of God's creation. While the fall of humanity perverted and distorted God's original intention, God seeks constantly to heal this brokenness and to restore all creation.

3 A contemporary prayer, used in some services of Morning Prayer, articulates Wesley's view of God succinctly: New every morning is your love, great God of light, and all day long you are working for good in the world. A common call and response in some churches today expresses the same vision: God is good. All the time. All the time. God is good. This affirmation of God's goodness and God's work for good at all times stands in stark contrast to the view of God held by many who think of God as authoritarian, critical, and distant. Wesley views God as the benevolent source of all love who always seeks to cooperate with, affirm, and come near to everyone and everything in creation.

☐ The True God

The eternal, almighty, all-wise, all-gracious God is the Creator of heaven and earth. God called the whole universe into being out of nothing by an all-powerful Word, all that is.[1] "Thus the heavens and the earth were created and all the hosts of them." And after God had set everything else in array, the plants after their kinds, fish and fowl, beasts and reptiles, after their kinds, God created human beings after God's own image. And the Lord saw that every distinct part of the universe was good. But when God saw everything the Word had made, all in connection with each other, "behold it was very good."[2]

And as this all-wise, all-gracious Being created all things, so God sustains all things. God is the preserver as well as the creator of everything that exists....

God is infinite in wisdom as well as in power, and all God's wisdom is continually employed in managing all the affairs of the creation for the good of all creatures.[3] For God's wisdom and goodness go hand in hand. They are inseparably united and continually act in concert with almighty power for the real good of all God's creatures. God's power, being equal to God's wisdom and goodness, continually co-operates with them. And to God all things are possible. God does whatever pleases, in heaven and earth and in the sea and all deep places. And we cannot doubt of God's exerting all power as in sustaining so in governing all that God has made.

JW SERMON "ON DIVINE PROVIDENCE" (1786),
8–9, 14 (*WORKS*, 2:537–38, 540)

☩ In 1745 Charles Wesley published a collection of hymns to be used for the celebration of Christmas, the *Nativity Hymns*. These hymns provide a window into his primary conceptions of God.

4 Note the parallelism here with John Wesley's descriptions of God in the previous selection.

5 In both these stanzas, Charles uses the images of "stooping," "dropping," and even "emptying" to describe the character of God. In the second person of the Trinity, Christ, God comes down to our level, enters into our world, and demonstrates the lengths to which love will go to establish and nurture relationships of love.

6 The true God desires union with all humanity. The purpose of creation was to celebrate relationships of love. God seeks the restoration of this goal above all things.

7 The mystery to which Charles refers is the glory of God. He alludes to St. Paul's discussion of the mystery long hidden, but now revealed: "And even if our gospel is veiled, it is veiled to those who are perishing. In their case the god of this world has blinded the minds of the unbelievers, to keep them from seeing the light of the gospel of the glory of Christ, who is the image of God.... For it is the God who said, 'Let light shine out of darkness,' who has shone in our hearts to give the light of the knowledge of the glory of God in the face of Jesus Christ" (2 Corinthians 4:3–4, 6). Nothing reflects God's glory more than the fully restored human life.

All-wise, all-good, Almighty Lord,[4]
Jesus, by highest heaven adored,
  Ere time its course began,
How did your glorious mercy stoop
To take the fallen nature up,
  When you became a man?

The eternal God from heaven came down,
The King of Glory dropped his crown,
  And veiled his majesty,
Emptied of all but love he came;
Jesus, I call you by your name
  Your pity bore for me.[5]

Did you not in your person join
The natures human and divine,
  That God and man might be
Henceforth inseparably one?[6]
Haste then, and make your nature known
  Incarnated in me.

O Christ, my hope, make known in me
The great, the glorious mystery,
  The hidden life impart.[7]
Come, O desire of nations, come,
Formed in a spotless virgin's womb,
  A pure believing heart.

CW HYMN "ALL-WISE, ALL-GOOD, ALMIGHTY LORD"
(NATIVITY HYMNS [1745], 19–20, HYMN 15, STANZAS 1–2, 4, 7)

✠ Charles Wesley's hymn celebrates the three persons of the Trinity, the God who creates, redeems, and sustains all life. Confronted with the reality of this God of Love, the child of God responds with praise, gratitude, and adoration. This song extends throughout all time.

1 Wesley quotes directly from Acts 17:28: "For 'in him we live, and move, and have our being'; as certain also of your own poets have said, 'For we are also his offspring.'" The setting of this statement is St. Paul's proclamation of the gospel in Athens. In an effort to establish a connection with his Greek listeners, he indicates that both Jesus and the great poets of the Greco-Roman world point to the same God.

2 The second person of the Trinity, the incarnate deity—Jesus—puts a song in the hearts of those who embrace his love and grace. Charles often uses this musical metaphor to explain the nature of the God known in Jesus.

☐ Trinity

Father, in whom we live,
    In whom we are and move,[1]
The glory, power, and praise receive
    Of thy creating love.
    Let all the angel-throng
    Give thanks to God on high,
While earth repeats the joyful song,
    And echoes to the sky.

Incarnate deity,
    Let all the ransomed race
Render in thanks their lives to thee
    For thy redeeming grace;
    The grace to sinners showed,
    Ye heavenly choirs proclaim,
And cry Salvation to our God,
    Salvation to the Lamb.[2]

Spirit of holiness,
    Let all thy saints adore
Thy sacred energy, and bless
    Thine heart-renewing power.
    Not angel-tongues can tell
    Thy love's ecstatic height,
The glorious joy unspeakable,
    The beatific sight.

CW hymn "To the Trinity"
(*Redemption Hymns* [1747], 44–45, Hymn 34, stanzas 1–3)

1 He refers here to the writer of Proverbs (16:4).

2 This theme of happiness pervades the work of John Wesley. Happiness, or blessedness, characterizes the lives of all who are properly rooted in God.

3 Wesley quotes directly from the *Confessions* of St. Augustine (I.1.1). One of the most cited texts from all of Augustine's works, this view of life shaped Wesley deeply; along with St. Augustine, the great Latin theologian of the early church in North Africa, he was convinced that the life of faith is a way of devotion, a perennial journey on the way to God.

4 Charles Wesley places great emphasis on the connection between creation and the "Word." In this stanza, he uses the term "word" four times. In the Prologue to John's Gospel, the evangelist elevates this conception of the "Word," linking it both to the person of Jesus and to creation: "In the beginning was the Word, and the Word was with God, and the Word was God. He was in the beginning with God. All things came into being through him, and without him not one thing came into being" (John 1:1–2).

☐ Creator

God "made all things," as the wise man observes, "for himself";[1] for "his glory they were created." Not "as if he needed anything," seeing "he giveth to all life, and breath, and all things." God made all things to be happy. God made man and women to be happy in themselves.[2] God is the proper center of spirits, for whom every created spirit was made. So true is that well-known saying of the ancient fathers: "Thou hast made us for thyself; and our heart cannot rest till it resteth in thee."[3]

JW SERMON "THE UNITY OF THE DIVINE BEING" (1789), 9 (*WORKS*, 4:63–64)

Let all that breathe, Jehovah praise,
  Almighty all-creating Lord,
Let earth and heaven God's power confess,
  Brought out of nothing by the Word!
God spoke the Word and it was done,
  The universe God's Word obeyed;
God's Word is the eternal Son,
  And Christ the whole creation made.[4]

CW HYMN "LET ALL THAT BREATHE, JEHOVAH PRAISE"
(*HYMNS FOR CHILDREN* [1763], 79, HYMN 90, STANZA 1)

1 John Wesley affirms a simple point: all are blessed who come to know God as "the parent of all good."

2 Wesley appreciated the importance of catechesis—instruction in the faith for all people, but for children in particular. In this sermon "On Family Religion," he discusses the way to instruct children about God. The principle he lays down guides his thinking about all theology: use plain words for plain people. The instruction that follows undergirds a vision of a great and loving God, who relates to us in the same way that a loving parent would care for a precious child.

☐ Parent of All Good

How truly wise are those who believe!... They know God—their Creator and friend—the parent of all good, the center of the spirits of all flesh, the sole happiness of all intelligent beings.[1]

JW SERMON "UPON OUR LORD'S SERMON ON THE MOUNT, XIII" (1750),
II.2 (WORKS, 1:692)

Speaking to your children early will be meaningless unless you likewise speak to them plainly. Use such words as little children may understand, just such as they use themselves. Carefully observe the few ideas that they have already and endeavor to graft what you say upon them. To take a little example, bid the child look up, and ask, "What do you see there?" "The sun." "See how bright it is! Feel how warm it shines upon your hand! Look, how it makes the grass and the flowers grow and the trees and everything look green! But God (though you cannot see God) is above the sky, and is a deal brighter than the sun! It is God ... that made the sun and you and me and everything. It is God that makes the grass and the flowers grow, that makes the trees green, and the fruit to come upon them! Think what God can do! God can do whatever God pleases. God can strike me or you dead in a moment. But God loves you. God loves to do you good. God loves to make you happy. Should not you then love God! You love me because I love you and do you good. But it is God that makes me love you. Therefore you should love God. And God will teach you how to love."[2]

JW SERMON "ON FAMILY RELIGION" (1783), III.7 (WORKS, 3:340–41)

1 In 1739 controversy provoked one of John Wesley's most famous sermons, "Free Grace." The sermon was a diatribe, in fact, against one of his close friends and colleagues, George Whitefield, who had embraced a Calvinistic understanding of salvation in which God's predestination of the faithful figured prominently. What disturbed Wesley the most in this teaching was the notion that the atoning work of Jesus—God's grace—was limited to those chosen for salvation by God, a logical necessity in this deterministic theology. Wesley found this not only repugnant but also antithetical to his view of God. In this sermon, therefore, he articulates a view of God's grace as a gift made available to all and in all. One of the central ideas that runs like a unifying thread throughout the whole of Wesley's theology is the understanding that all people—indeed, all creation—is enveloped by the wooing activity of God's grace. God surrounds and fills everyone and everything with grace. No one stands outside the possibility of this loving embrace.

2 John appended one of Charles's very lengthy hymns on "universal redemption" to his published sermon. The central argument that runs through the lyrical text affirms that God's grace extends to all and that those who respond to that grace in faith will be saved. Charles articulates a third alternative, in other words, to a radical doctrine of election, on one hand, in which only a few are saved, and a radical doctrine of universal salvation, on the other, in which everyone will be saved. This stanza emphasizes the universal extent of God's grace and God's embrace of all people in Jesus.

☐ Free Grace for All

How freely does God love the world! While we were yet sinners, "Christ died for the ungodly." While we were "dead in sin," God "spared not his own Son, but delivered him up for us all." And how "freely with him" does God "give us all things!" Verily, free grace is all in all!

The grace or love of God—the source of our salvation—is free in all, and free for all.[1]

JW SERMON "FREE GRACE" (1739), 1–2 (WORKS, 3:544)

Mercy I sing, transporting sound,
  The joy of earth and heaven!
Mercy, by every sinner found,
  Who takes what God hath given.

Mercy for all thy hands have made,
  Immense, and unconfined,
Throughout thine every work displayed,
  Embracing humankind.[2]

CW HYMN "UNIVERSAL REDEMPTION"
(HSP [1740], 136, STANZAS 4–5,
APPENDED TO JW SERMON "FREE GRACE")

⊹ Both John and Charles Wesley articulate a vision of universal redemption throughout their voluminous writings. These two selections represent, perhaps, their most vehement attacks on those who seek to limit the range of God's redemptive work in Jesus. John's *Predestination Calmly Considered* and Charles's whole collection of *Hymns on God's Everlasting Love* rail against what they consider to be the unbiblical teachings of irresistible grace—the view that God's saving grace is applied to those whom God has determined to save (the elect) without any response to it on their part—and the predestination of the elect. We will explore these issues more fully in the section on the Wesleyan "way of salvation" that follows (see p. 97). The most important issue for the Wesleys in this controversy could be formulated as a question: What kind of God does your doctrine of salvation reveal? They could not square their doctrine of a God of love and grace with the view of a God limited by the logic of predestination.

1 Wesley battles his Calvinistic opponents here. By "election" he means God's unilateral choice of those who are saved. Alternatively, "reprobation" refers to God's unilateral choice of those who are damned. He was opposed to any view of salvation that minimized or denied a dynamic and mutual relationship between God and God's children.

☐ Universal Redemption

Election and reprobation are completely inconsistent with the truth and sincerity of God![1] In particular, they are antithetical to the scriptural account of God's love and goodness, those attributes which God peculiarly claims, wherein God glories above all the rest. It is not written, "God is justice," or "God is truth" (although God is just and true in all God's ways). But it is written, "God is love," love in the abstract, without bounds, and "there is no end of his goodness." God's love extends even to those who neither love nor fear God. God is good even to the evil and the unthankful, yea, without any exception or limitation, to all God's children. For the Lord is loving (or good) to everyone, and God's mercy is over all God's works.

JW *Predestination Calmly Considered* (1752),
42 (*Works* [Jackson], 10:227)

2   I have preserved the italics of the original. This reveals Charles's pervasive emphasis on the salvation of God offered to "all." God extends free, everlasting love to all. Christ died for all. God reaches out to everyone with sufficient, sovereign, saving grace. All can hope. God draws all. "Preventing grace"—grace that precedes everything else—is free for all.

Father, whose *everlasting love*
  Thy only Son for sinners gave,
Whose grace *to all* did *freely* move,
  And sent him down a *world to save.*

Help us thy mercy to extol,
  Immense, unfathomed, unconfined;
To praise the Lamb who *died for all,*
  The *Savior of all humankind.*

Thy *undistinguishing* regard
  Was cast on Adam's fallen race;
For all thou hast in Christ prepared
  Sufficient, sovereign, saving grace.

Jesus hath said, we *all* shall hope;
  Preventing grace for all is free;
"And I, if I be lifted up,
  I will *draw all folk* unto me."[2]

CW HYMN "FATHER, WHOSE EVERLASTING LOVE"
(*HYMNS ON GOD'S EVERLASTING LOVE* [1741], 3, HYMN 1:1–4)

1 Charles Wesley composed hundreds of hymns on the Incarnation. In these expressions of lyrical theology, he describes Jesus, the second person of the Trinity, as the friend of humanity. In Jesus, God enters human history, comes close, lives with us (Immanuel means "God with us"), and offers friendship to every person. Wesley never wavered from this central conviction, that the act of the Incarnation reveals the character of God's transforming friendship and love.

2 More often than not, in order to explain the mystery of God becoming human in Jesus, Wesley employs the concept of *kenosis*, or self-emptying, drawn from an early Christian hymn quoted in St. Paul's Letter to the Philippians (2:5–11). He often says that in the person of Jesus, God "emptied himself of all but love." Through the Incarnation, in other words, God relinquished all those characteristics we generally associate with the Divine—omnipotence, omniscience, omnipresence—without compromising the core essence of the divine nature, namely, love.

3 Wesley continues his exploration of the mystery of the Incarnation in this powerful couplet. The God who created all that is enters time and space in the form of a human baby. How can this paradox be fully understood? The One who is eternal, the Alpha and Omega, the beginning and the end who was and is and is to come, enters the stream of history in a particular place and moment in time; eternity itself becomes temporal. All thoughtful people bow before this mystery, filled with awe and wonder.

☐ Incarnate Love

Glory be to God on high,
   And peace on earth descend;
God comes down and bows the sky,
   And shows himself our friend!**1**
God the invisible *appears*,
   God the blest, the great I AM
Sojourns in this vale of tears,
   And Jesus is his name.

Him the angels all adored,
   Their Maker and their King;
Tidings of their humbled Lord
   They now to mortals bring.
Emptied of his majesty,**2**
   Of his dazzling glories shorn,
Being's source *begins* to be,
   And God himself is BORN!**3**

CW HYMN "GLORY BE TO GOD ON HIGH"
(*NATIVITY HYMNS* [1745], 5–6, HYMN 4, STANZAS 1–2)

✠ In this hymn, Charles Wesley connects the Incarnation with its primary purpose—the atonement of all and reconciliation with God. Jesus comes to save, but because unique individuals appropriate this work, no single theory of atonement suffices for him. His doctrine of the redemptive work of Jesus is richly textured, reflecting all the classical theories drawn from various strands of the biblical witness. His reference to Jesus taking the sin of humanity upon himself sounds very much like a substitionary or satisfaction theory of atonement, the view that Jesus dies as a substitute for others. His theology reflects a deep concern for the effects of sin and the brokenness that characterizes all people. His conception of Jesus' victory over death reflects a more ancient *Christus victor* theme—the view that Jesus' death overcomes the powers of evil—as does his reference to the metaphor of ransom and release. Drawing images primarily from the apostle Paul, his vision of redemption entails our victory, through Jesus, over all those powers that separate us from God's love and God's loving ways—particularly sin, death, and evil. He alludes to the moral influence theory of atonement in his explication of "love divine" and its implied power to transform. Built originally upon the teachings of Abelard, this theory maintains that Jesus died to bring positive moral change to humanity. According to Charles, God must find some way to turn human beings around so as to fix their attention on what really matters in life. Nothing has greater transformative power than the revelation of God's love in the self-sacrifice of Jesus on the cross, where Jesus gives his life for his friends. As in many other areas of his theology, Wesley reveals a synthesizing approach that refuses a simplistic or reductionistic understanding of the ways of God.

☐ The Work of Christ

What shall I do my God to love,
  My Savior and the world's to praise?
Whose kindness and compassion move
  To me and all the fallen race;
Whose mercy is divinely free
For all the fallen race and me.

I long to know and to make known
  The height and depth of love divine,
The kindness thou to me hast shown,
  Whose every sin was counted thine;
My God for me resigned his breath,
He died to save my soul from death.

All souls are thine; and thou for all
  The ransom of thy life hast given,
To raise all sinners from the fall,
  And bring them back to God and heaven,
Thou all the world hast died to save,
And all may thy salvation have.

CW HYMN "DESIRING TO LOVE" (*HSP* [1742], 24–25, STANZAS 1–3)

1 John Wesley is drawing here on a longstanding tradition in Western theology (owing much to John Calvin) that conceived Jesus' work through the lens of his offices as prophet, priest, and king. While Wesley was concerned about how to properly interpret the "past" or "finished" work of Jesus—his redemptive work that made atonement possible—he emphasized with equal or even greater vigor the "present" work of Jesus. Despite the foundational nature of "Christ dying for us," he was equally concerned about "Christ reigning in us." In other words, he did not view atonement as the totality of Jesus' redemptive work; rather, he viewed the cross as the foundation of God's present and transforming work through Jesus in the life of the believer.

Following the order of the offices that Wesley seems to have preferred (reflected in the sermon from which this excerpt is drawn), Jesus' role as priest precedes his other work of restoration in our lives. We never outgrow our need for Jesus as priest. We receive God's pardon through his priestly office. But God not only offers forgiveness; God also delivers those who trust in Jesus from the power of sin. As prophet, Jesus reveals the moral image that God intends for us all. Jesus restores our awareness of God's law and initiates the renewal of Christlike character. Jesus the king leads us toward that recovery. The present work of Jesus comes to its full fruition, then, through the office of Jesus as king. Jesus as Lord rules in all believing hearts and enables full conformity to his own image as the believer grows into the fullest possible love of God and neighbor.

Jesus not only saves through dying on the cross and thereby procuring our forgiveness, but his redemptive work also includes our growth into holiness of heart and life. Jesus as priest forgives; as prophet guides; as king restores.

It is our part thus to preach Christ, by preaching everything that he has revealed. We may indeed, without blame, yea, and with a peculiar blessing from God, declare the love of our Lord Jesus Christ. We may speak in a more special manner of "the Lord our righteousness." We may expatiate upon the grace of God in Christ "reconciling the world unto himself." We may, at proper opportunities, dwell upon God's praise, as "bearing the iniquities of us all, as wounded for our transgressions, and bruised for our iniquities, that by his stripes we might be healed." But still we should not preach Christ according to his word if we were wholly to confine ourselves to this. We must ... proclaim Christ in all his offices.[1] To preach Christ as a workman that needs not to be ashamed is to preach him, not only as our great *High Priest*, "taken from among men, and ordained for men, in things pertaining to God," as such, "reconciling us to God by his blood" and "ever living to make intercession for us"— but likewise as the *Prophet of the Lord*, "who of God is made unto us wisdom," who, by his word and his Spirit, is with us always, "guiding us into all truth";—yea, and as remaining a *King* forever, as giving laws to all whom he has bought with his blood, as restoring those to the image of God whom he had first reinstated in his favor, as reigning in all believing hearts until he has "subdued all things to himself,"—until he hath utterly cast out all sin and brought in everlasting righteousness.

JW SERMON "THE LAW ESTABLISHED THROUGH FAITH, II" (1750),
I.6 (*WORKS*, 2:37–38)

✝ The Wesleys equated the Holy Spirit—the third person of the Trinity—with God's empowering presence. They placed the Spirit at the very center of their understanding of the Christian life. It is through the gracious presence and power of the Spirit that all people come to know who God is, are restored in their relationship with God, and develop those virtues, or fruits, that characterize the children of God. In this hymn, Charles explores the various dimensions of the Spirit's work as comforter, teacher, guide, peacemaker, catalyst, and physician.

1 Wesley assumes that fallen human beings must be taught the will of God. This is not something that comes naturally. In the same way, the Spirit must teach us how to love, and this learning takes place in the context of the community of faith, gathered around the Word (scripture) and the Table (Eucharist). The Spirit interprets God's ways and God's will and guides the children of God into all truth.

2 Only when we are teachable can the Spirit shape our lives. Whenever we open up our minds and hearts, however, to the work of the Holy Spirit, God can help us internalize the law of love. No longer something imposed on us from the outside, it becomes an internal guidance mechanism, directing all we say and do.

3 The Spirit imparts God's promises to us. Love, joy, and peace are the Spirit's greatest gifts, the core virtues of our inheritance in Jesus.

☐ The Work of the Spirit

Jesus, we on the words depend
  Spoken by thee while present here,
The Father in my name shall send
  The Holy Ghost, the Comforter.

THAT PROMISE made to Adam's race,
  Now, Lord, in us, even us fulfill,
And give the Spirit of thy grace,
  To teach us all thy perfect will.[1]

That teacher of all humankind,
  That guide infallible impart,
To bring thy sayings to our mind,
  And write them on our faithful heart.[2]

The length and breadth of love reveal,
  The height and depth of deity,
And all the sons of glory seal,
  And change and make us all like thee![3]

CW HYMN "JOHN XIV. 25, 26, 27"
(*WHITSUNDAY HYMNS* [1746], 15, HYMN 12, STANZAS 1–3, 6)

✢ In 1762 Charles Wesley wrote three one-stanza hymns based on Exodus 34:6: "The Lord passed before him, and proclaimed, 'The Lord, the Lord, a God merciful and gracious, slow to anger, and abounding in steadfast love and faithfulness.'" The Wesleys celebrated a God of pure, unbounded love and grace. Charles describes that love as ceaseless and unexhausted, unmerited and free, faithful and constant, unalterably sure. Likewise, God's truth and goodness are unfathomable and plenteous. This God delights, helps, waits, saves. Moreover, the full energy of God's love and grace extends to every creature, "enough for all, enough for each, enough for evermore." The Wesley brothers poured all their energies into the proclamation of this good news.

☐ Pure, Unbounded Love

Thy ceaseless unexhausted love,
  Unmerited and free,
Delights our evil to remove,
  And help our misery;
Thou waitest to be gracious still,
  Thou dost with sinners bear,
That saved, we may thy goodness feel,
  And all thy grace declare.

Thy goodness and thy truth to me,
  To every soul abound,
A vast unfathomable sea,
  Where all our thoughts are drowned;
Its streams the whole creation reach,
  So plenteous is the store,
Enough for all, enough for each,
  Enough for evermore.

Faithful, O Lord, thy mercies are,
  A rock that cannot move,
A thousand promises declare
  Thy constancy of love.
Throughout the universe it reigns
  Unalterably sure,
And while the truth of God remains,
  The goodness must endure.

CW HYMNS "GRACIOUS, LONG-SUFFERING," "ABUNDANT IN GOODNESS,"
AND "ABUNDANT IN TRUTH," ALL EXPOSITIONS OF EXODUS 34:6
(SCRIPTURE HYMNS [1762], 1:53–54, HYMNS 169–71)

PART THREE
The Way of Salvation

☩ Martin Luther centered his theology on the cross of Christ. John Calvin oriented his theological vision around the concept of God's sovereignty. For the Wesleys, most everything revolved around the way of salvation. This may have been the case, in part, because most people's questions about faith relate, in one way or another, to the meaning of life and how Jesus provides the key to answering the questions of salvation and ultimate meaning. The Wesleys' theology cannot be summed up entirely by their doctrine of salvation, but the way in which they find their way to God through Jesus informs all their questions about life.

Salvation, for the Wesleys, is a process. Although there may be critical experiences or turning points in the path, the journey to God is the most important thing. A pilgrimage is not static; it is dynamic and always moving. This particular pilgrimage is extremely personal. Intimacy with self, others, and God characterizes it through and through. It is a dynamic, relational process leading to holiness of heart and life—true happiness.

1 John Wesley provides this helpful metaphor to understand the way of salvation. The three primary components of redemption—repentance, faith, and holiness—define the Christian journey as homecoming. Through Jesus we find our way home. Every home is different, of course, and Wesley's use of this image in no way prescribes a one-size-fits-all approach to salvation. Indeed, all must find their own way, follow their own course; therefore, all experience the homeward pilgrimage in different ways. But the Wesleys do believe that these three elements are essential to the journey.

☐ A Dynamic Relational Process

I have again and again, with all the plainness I could, declared what our constant doctrines are whereby we are distinguished only from heathens or nominal Christians; not from any that worship God in spirit and in truth. Our main doctrines which include all the rest are three, that of repentance, of faith, and of holiness. The first of these we account, as it were, the porch of religion; the next, the door; the third, religion itself.[1]

JW *THE PRINCIPLES OF A METHODIST FARTHER EXPLAINED* (1745),
VI.4 (*WORKS* [JACKSON], 8:472)

⊹ John Wesley provides the most succinct description of the way of salvation in his sermon "On Working Out Our Own Salvation." This is a lovely summary of critical insights, events, and turning points in our relationship with God. As you can see from this paragraph, salvation is grace upon grace. Grace is central. Wesley even gives specific names to the ways in which grace functions in our lives. First and foremost, he does not conceive grace as a thing; rather, the Wesleys speak of grace in relational categories. Grace envelopes, or surrounds, every person. That is what he means by "prevenient, or preventing grace," or grace that comes before anything else. It is God reaching out to us in love. Wesley next connects "convincing grace" with repentance. Whenever we stand in the presence of God, we are convinced about how far we are from what God intends us to be. With God's light shining on us and into our hearts, we realize how far from home we are. God declares us to be forgiven in Christ, a pardon we experience through "justifying grace." Having experienced God's unconditional love, we then yearn to grow into the fullest possible love of God and others, assisted in that quest by "sanctifying grace." Although given different names, grace is grace is grace. Grace is nothing other than God's lavish, generous, unconditional love poured out on us. God expresses that love in different ways, given where we are in our relationship with Jesus. Regardless, God's grace is ever present to enlighten, to convince, to pardon, and to love us.

2 | Wesleyan theology is conjunctive; that means it is a both/and way of looking at life, not an either/or approach. Here we have just one of several conjunctions in this paragraph that explicates the way of salvation: justification and sanctification. Salvation, in other words, is both forgiveness and restoration. Through Jesus, God forgives our sins but also begins the process of restoring Jesus' image in us. We are saved by faith in Jesus, but we also live into the deepest possible love. Faith working by love leads to holiness of heart and life.

Salvation begins with what is usually termed (and very properly) "preventing grace," including the first wish to please God, the first dawn of light concerning God's will, and the first slight, transient conviction of having sinned against God. All these imply some tendency toward life, some degree of salvation, the beginning of a deliverance from a blind, unfeeling heart, quite insensible of God and the things of God. Salvation is carried on by "convincing grace," usually in scripture termed "repentance," which brings a larger measure of self-knowledge and a farther deliverance from the heart of stone. Afterwards we experience the proper Christian salvation whereby "through grace" we "are saved by faith," consisting of those two grand branches, justification and sanctification.[2]

(continued on page 103)

3 Here is another conjunction. The journey of salvation is both instantaneous and gradual. There are critical events and turning points, but the journey as a whole is as important as those special moments. We have mountaintop experiences, but a path leads us both up the mountain and down the other side into mission and service in the world.

4 The Wesleys believe that balance is the key to life. The Christian life is faith and works, crisis and process, individual and social, and it all leads to love.

✠ Isaac Watts, the father of the English hymn, said that this one hymn of Charles Wesley was worth all the verse that he himself had ever written. Expounding on Genesis 32:24–32, "Wrestling Jacob" is both a profound lyrical exposition of the way of salvation and a spiritual autobiography. Only several of the most critical verses are quoted here from the hymn of fourteen stanzas.

5 Wesley's questions are poignant. Who is God? What is God's nature? Can I know God? These are our questions as well.

By justification we are saved from the guilt of sin and restored to the favor of God. By sanctification we are saved from the power and root of sin and restored to the image of God. All experience as well as scripture shows this salvation to be both instantaneous and gradual.[3] It begins the moment we are justified in the holy, humble, gentle, patient love of God and humanity. It gradually increases from that moment as a "grain of mustard seed, which at first is the least of all seeds, but" gradually "puts forth large branches," and becomes a great tree, till, in another instant the heart is cleansed from all sin and filled with pure love to God and neighbor. But even that love increases more and more till we "grow up in all things into him that is our head," "till we attain the measure of the stature of the fullness of Christ."[4]

JW SERMON "ON WORKING OUT OUR OWN SALVATION" (1785),
II.1 (*WORKS*, 3:203–4)

Come, O thou Traveler unknown,
　Whom still I hold, but cannot see!
My company before is gone,
　And I am left alone with thee;
With thee all night I mean to stay
And wrestle till the break of day.

I need not tell thee who I am,
　My misery and sin declare;
Thyself hast called me by my name,
　Look on thy hands and read it there.
But who, I ask thee, who art thou?
Tell me thy name, and tell me now.[5]

(*continued on page 105*)

6 Take special note of the paradox here. Each of us yearns to know God. We struggle and wrestle with God in our effort to make sense of life. Grace leads us to the point at which we know we can answer none of the questions that plague us. Only God can answer those questions, fulfill our need, do for us what we cannot do for ourselves. Grace enables us "to let go and to let God." In his frequent discussions of Wesleyan doctrine, one scholar, Robert Cushman, described this death of human effort as the "inactivation of the will through despair." The paradox is that we find God by letting go. We find our way home by giving up on our own quest. We relinquish all to God, entrust our lives to Jesus, and experience God's unconditional love. God loved us in the beginning, loves us in the present moment, and will never stop loving us into the future.

7 This pivotal stanza marks the critical breakthrough. Having demanded to know God's nature and name, God reveals the central reality of all life: "'Tis love, 'tis love! Thou diedst for me." The wrestler knows that God is love, but not in a theoretical, generic sense; the seeker knows that God loves him or her because of the way in which Jesus reveals that love in such a remarkable and unimaginable way. God does not coerce love—indeed, love can never be forced—but speaks love into the heart, liberates the soul, and establishes a life-giving relationship that will never end.

8 Whenever the Wesleys published this hymn, they printed the words UNIVERSAL LOVE in full capitals. This is the heart, the center, of the Christian faith. God is pure universal love.

9 All of the remaining stanzas of the hymn, subsequent to the liberating realization of God's unconditional love in this verse, conclude with this simple but triumphant declaration.

10 Here is the homecoming image yet again.

Yield to me now—for I am weak
  But confident in self-despair![6]
Speak to my heart, in blessing speak,
  Be conquered by my instant prayer:
Speak, or thou never hence shalt move,
And tell me, if thy name is Love.

Tis Love! 'tis Love! thou diedst for me,[7]
  I hear thy whisper in my heart.
The morning breaks, the shadows flee,
  Pure UNIVERSAL LOVE thou art:[8]
To me, to all, thy mercies move—
Thy nature, and thy name is Love.[9]

Lame as I am, I take the prey,
  Hell, earth, and sin with ease overcome;
I leap for joy, pursue my way,
  And as a bounding hart fly home,[10]
Through all eternity to prove
Thy nature, and thy name is Love.

CW HYMN "WRESTLING JACOB" (HSP [1742],
115–18, STANZAS 1–2, 8–9, 14)

✠ Repentance is the first great movement of the way of salvation. The Greek word in the Christian Scriptures, from which this term comes, means "to be turned around." The same word can be translated as "conversion." Repentance, therefore, is a course-altering experience. This turning is God's action upon us, but it cannot be achieved unless we are fully involved.

1 Are human beings by nature good or evil? How you answer this fundamental question—good, evil, or both—determines how you think about everything else in life. The view that John Wesley supports here is usually described as the doctrine of original sin. In other words, all people are by nature evil. He wrote a lengthy treatise on this subject in which he described the broken nature of the human being. For him, this did not mean that everything a person does is evil, that there is no good in humanity whatsoever; rather, it means that this brokenness touches every aspect of our life—the way we think, feel, and act. While this might seem like an extreme view, we will see how Wesley adjusts it as we move through the way of salvation.

2 Wesley alludes here to Jesus' conversation with Nicodemus (John 3:1–10) about his need to be born again, or born from above.

☐ Repentance

Human Brokenness

And "in Adam all died," all humankind, all the children of earth who were then in Adam's loins. The natural consequence of this is that everyone descended from him comes into the world spiritually dead, dead to God, wholly "dead in sin," entirely void of the life of God, void of the image of God, of all that "righteousness and holiness" wherein Adam was created.[1] Instead of this every person born into the world now bears the image of the devil in pride and self-will—the image of the beast in sensual appetites and desires. This then is the foundation of the new birth—the entire corruption of our nature. Hence it is that being "born in sin" we "must be born again." Hence everyone that is born of a woman must be born of the Spirit of God.[2]

JW SERMON "THE NEW BIRTH" (1760), I.4 (WORKS, 2:190)

3 This language is harsh to modern ears. During the time of the Wesleys, the terms "heathenism" and "heathen" referred to ancient philosophical or religious systems and those who adhered to them. In this particular document, John actually imported these statements from an older seventeenth-century treatise related to this issue of original sin. Unlike many Christians of his day, however, he embraced truth wherever he found it, but he also believed that many people fall into the trap of self-delusion if they do not acknowledge their own broken condition.

4 In his sermon "Original Sin," Wesley maintains a pessimistic view of the human person. He draws his conclusion about the condition of humanity not only from his reading of scripture but also from his observation of life and human history. His ultimate conclusion: something is seriously wrong with the human creature; God must do for us what we cannot do for ourselves if we are to be healed or renewed. In particular, the human disease of preoccupation with self can only be healed by some external force that both cures and reorients the child to the loving, parent God and away from self. The only force that can heal the human condition is love.

We may learn one grand, fundamental difference between Christianity, considered as a system of doctrines, and the most refined heathenism. Many of the ancient heathens have largely described the vices of particular people.[3] They have spoken much against their covetousness or cruelty, their luxury, or prodigality. Some have dared to say that "no man is born without vices of one kind or another." But still, as none of them were apprised of the fall of humanity, so none of them knew our total corruption. They knew not that all people were empty of all good and filled with all manner of evil. They were wholly ignorant of the entire depravation of the whole human nature, of every person born into the world, in every faculty of his or her soul, not so much by those particular vices which reign in particular persons as by the general flood of atheism and idolatry, of pride, self-will, and love of the world. This, therefore, is the first, grand, distinguishing point between heathenism and Christianity. The one acknowledges that many people are infected with many vices and even born with a proneness to them, but supposes regardless that in some the natural good much overbalances the evil. The other declares that all people are "conceived in sin" and "shaped in wickedness," that hence there is in every person a "carnal mind which is enmity against God, which is not, cannot be, subject to his law," and which so infects the whole soul that "there dwelleth in him, in his flesh," in the natural state, "no good thing," but "all the imagination of the thoughts of his heart is evil," "only evil," and that "continually."[4]

JW SERMON "ORIGINAL SIN" (1759), III.1 (*WORKS*, 2:182–83)

5   Charles Wesley pulls no punches with regard to the fallen condition of humanity either. The "great mountain" to which he refers here is sin. Like St. Anselm—famed Archbishop of Canterbury (1033–1109) and author of the earliest known treatise on atonement, *Why the God-Human?*—he says in essence: *You have not yet considered how great a weight sin is.* He takes sin with utmost seriousness.

6   Note the way Wesley describes sin here. Essentially, sin is the absence of light—darkness and perversity. His poetic language of "love inordinate" is reminiscent of St. Augustine's view of "disordered affections" in the human being. Our problem is not that we do not love; rather, the primary issue is that we love in the wrong way. Instead of loving God as an end or ultimate goal, we love God as a means to our own ends. God must reorder our affections or loves. Wesley further demonstrates how sin manifests itself most fully in our anger, lust, and pride.

7   Charles recognized the depth of sin. This is no superficial thing, but reaches into the deepest parts of our being. Sin lurks deep within.

O great mountain, who art thou
  Immense, immoveable!
High as heaven aspires thy brow,
  Thy foot sinks deep as hell.
Thee, alas! I long have known,
  Long have felt thee fixed within,
Still beneath thy weight I groan;
  Thou art indwelling sin.[5]

Thou art darkness in my mind,
  Perverseness in my will,
Love inordinate and blind,
  Which always cleaves to ill;
Every passion's wild excess,
  Anger, lust, and pride thou art,
Self, and sin, and sinfulness,
  And unbelief of heart.[6]

CW HYMN ON ZECHARIAH 4:7 (*HSP* [1742],
234–35, HYMN 372, STANZAS 1–2)

Show me, as my soul can bear
  The depth of inbred sin,
All the unbelief declare,
  The pride that lurks within;[7]
Take me, whom thyself hast bought,
  Bring into captivity
Every high aspiring thought
  That would not stoop to thee.

CW HYMN "WAITING FOR CHRIST THE PROPHET"
(*HSP* [1742], 209, STANZA 5)

✢ In this hymn Wesley provides a lyrical exposition of Jesus' words recorded in Matthew 11 and one of his most masterful uses of anaphora, the literary device of repeating the same word at the beginning of consecutive lines. Wesley identifies the deepest desire of the human heart—rest—before describing the human state—weary and burdened. First he presents God's promise. He suggests the remedy before he offers his diagnosis, emphasizing God's prevenient action, God's desire to heal, and God's initiative rooted in grace. His description of the consequences of sin that we feel so deeply in our lives overwhelms us: *weary, weary, weary, weary. Burdened, burdened, burdened, burdened.*

In the same way that sin weighs us down completely, Wesley believes that the rest God offers in Jesus fully encompasses as well. When we abide in Jesus we are liberated from servitude, from toil and woe, from grief and fear. Wesley concludes with the astounding affirmation that forgiveness procures our rest. This act of God for us in Jesus frees us from the burden of feeling that we can never do enough to please God, others, or ourselves. It emancipates us from the weariness of our own efforts that are often life depleting.

The Burden of Sin

Come, ye weary sinners, come,
  All who groan to bear your load,
Jesus calls his wanderers home;
  Hasten to your pardoning God.
Come, ye guilty spirits oppressed,
  Answer to the Savior's call,
"Come, and I will give you rest,
  Come, and I will save you all."

Weary of this war within,
  Weary of this endless strife,
Weary of ourselves and sin,
  Weary of a wretched life;
Fain we would on thee rely,
  Cast on thee our sin and care,
To thy arms of mercy fly,
  Find our lasting quiet there.

Burdened with a world of grief,
  Burdened with our sinful load,
Burdened with this unbelief,
  Burdened with the wrath of God,
Lo! We come to thee for ease,
  True and gracious as thou art,
Now our groaning soul release,
  Write forgiveness on our heart.

CW HYMN "COME, YE WEARY SINNERS, COME"
(*REDEMPTION HYMNS* [1747], 12–13, HYMN 10, STANZAS 1, 3–4)

8 Long before the birth of modern psychology, Wesley defined prevenient grace primarily in terms of the conscience. His concern for the human conscience is something he learned from his mother. One of the most important goals of life for her was to maintain a conscience devoid of any offense to God. She wanted to be able to look God in the face, so to speak, to have no thoughts, actions, or words that separated her from God. She did everything she could to keep a clear conscience.

9 Wesley makes a fairly sophisticated argument here. If you argue that everyone has sinned and that there is nothing we can do about it (the Calvinist position), this would seem to absolve the guilt of all, since we cannot be held accountable for something over which we had no control (Calvin actually argues that we are still culpable, despite the fact we can do nothing other than sin). Wesley believes something quite different. First, all have sinned. All human beings are by nature evil. His starting point is the same as Calvin's or any of the other great sixteenth-century reformers. However, he believes that God would never leave us in this state because it makes love impossible. So God intervenes. Sinful though we are, God envelops us in God's love and grace. This "prevenient grace" enlightens us so that we are capable of recognizing our fallen condition. Moreover, this grace makes it possible for us to have a role in the relational process of restoration with God. None of us has an excuse, because God's grace enlightens every person.

10 This concluding sentence summarizes Wesley's main point. The grace to which he refers here is what he calls "prevenient grace" because it comes before everything else. None of us is without grace. God is reaching out to everyone. The question is not, *How do I access God's grace?* Rather, the question is: *How do I properly use the grace that already surrounds me in life?*

Prevenient Grace

If we take this in its utmost extent it will include all that is wrought in the soul by what is frequently termed "natural conscience," but more properly "preventing grace." This includes all the "drawings" of "the Father," the desires after God, which, if we yield to them increase more and more; all that "light" wherewith the Son of God "enlighteneth everyone that cometh into the world," showing every person "to do justly, to love mercy, and to walk humbly with his God"; all the convictions which God's Spirit from time to time works in every child of earth.[8]

JW SERMON "THE SCRIPTURE WAY OF SALVATION" (1765), I.2 (*WORKS*, 2:156–57)

Allowing that all people's souls are dead in sin by nature, this excuses none, seeing there is no one that is in a state of mere nature; no persons, unless they have quenched the Spirit, are wholly void of the grace of God.[9] No one living is entirely destitute of what is vulgarly called "natural conscience." But this is not natural; it is more properly termed "preventing grace." Everyone has a greater or lesser measure of this, which waits not for the call of anyone. Everyone has sooner or later good desires, although most people stifle them before they can strike deep root or produce any considerable fruit. Everyone has some measure of that light, some faint glimmering ray, which sooner or later, more or less, enlightens everyone that comes into the world. And all people, unless they are of the small number whose conscience is seared as with a hot iron, feels more or less uneasy when they act contrary to the light of their own conscience. So that none sin because they do not have grace, but because they do not use the grace that they have.[10]

JW SERMON "ON WORKING OUT OUR OWN SALVATION" (1785),
III.4 (*WORKS*, 3:207)

☩ Charles Wesley demonstrates how God extends grace to every person. He associates prevenient grace with the primary image of light. This grace is universal and universally operative. It touches everyone and everything God has created. This is the source of our responsibility in the process of salvation. We partner with God as we move in the direction of the light, and God's grace makes this partnership itself a possibility.

True light of the whole world, appear,
Answer in us thy character,
  Thou uncreated Sun;
Jesus, thy beams on all are shed,
That all may by thy beams be led
  To that eternal throne.

Lightened by thy interior ray
Thee every child of Adam may
  His unknown God adore,
And following close thy secret grace
Emerge into that glorious place
  Where darkness is no more.

The universal light thou art,
And turned to thee the darkest heart
  A glimmering spark may find;
Let man reject it or embrace,
Thou offerest once thy saving grace
  To me, and all mankind.

Light of my soul, I follow thee,
In humble faith on earth to see
  Thy perfect day of love,
And then with all thy saints in light
To gain the beatific sight
  Which makes their heaven above.

CW HYMN "TRUE LIGHT OF THE WHOLE WORLD, APPEAR"
(*SCRIPTURE HYMNS* [1762], 2:238–39, HYMN 400 ON JOHN 12:25–26)

✠ Repentance reveals both what we need to be saved *from* and what we need to be saved *into*. For the Wesleys, salvation is both legal and therapeutic; it is related both to Jesus' redemptive work *for* us and the Spirit's transforming work *in* us; it revolves around freedom from sin and freedom to love. Repentance, therefore, is like the threshold of a door that opens the way to our spiritual healing. It is like the first step in the journey that leads us home.

These two readings articulate the essence of repentance from a Wesleyan perspective. Jesus' parable of the prodigal son in Luke 15:11–32 provides both the image and the language for the Wesleys' vision of repentance. A son requested his inheritance, squandered all he had, and found himself miserable, alone, starving, dying, and lost. The critical turning point in the story comes with these important words: "But when he came to himself." John Wesley is the only theologian I have ever found to define repentance as "true self-understanding." That is the pervasive language of these excerpts. The prodigal son "came to himself." In the depth of his despair, he remembered who he was and to whom he belonged.

This rediscovery includes two critical dimensions. On the one hand, the prodigal son understood too well who he was in that moment. He realized how far he had strayed. He was overcome with a sense of guilt and shame. That discovery about himself broke his heart. On the other hand, he came to himself in the sense of acknowledging the one to whom he belonged, realizing that nothing could ever strip him of his primary and eternal identity. He would always be his father's son, regardless of his transgressions. His repentance, therefore, was both an act of contrition and an affirmation of identity. For the Wesleys, repentance is true self-understanding in this sense.

11 "Know yourself" was the ancient Greek philosopher Socrates's central rule of life.

True Self-Knowledge

Repent, that is, know yourselves.[11] This is the first repentance, previous to faith, even conviction or self-knowledge. Awake, then, you who are sleeping. Know yourself to be a sinner and what manner of sinner you are. Know that corruption of your inmost nature whereby you are very far gone from original righteousness, whereby "the flesh lusteth" always "contrary to the Spirit," through that "carnal mind which is enmity against God," which "is not subject to the law of God, neither indeed can be." Know that you are corrupted in every power, in every faculty of your soul, that you are totally corrupted in every one of these, all the foundations being out of course. The eyes of your understanding are darkened so that they cannot discern God or the things of God. The clouds of ignorance and error rest upon you and cover you with the shadow of death. You know nothing yet as you ought to know, neither God, nor the world, nor yourself. Your will is no longer the will of God, but is utterly perverse and distorted, averse from all good, from all which God loves, and prone to all evil, to every abomination which God hates. Your affections are alienated from God and scattered abroad over the earth. All your passions, both your desires and aversions, your joys and sorrows, your hopes and fears, are out of frame, are either inappropriate in their degree or placed on inappropriate objects. So that there is no soundness in your soul, but "from the crown of the head to the sole of the foot" (to use the strong expression of the prophet) there are only "wounds, and bruises, and putrefying sores."

JW SERMON "THE WAY TO THE KINGDOM" (1746), II.1 (*WORKS*, 1:225–26)

✠ In one of Charles Wesley's more familiar hymns, "Depth of Mercy," he plumbs the depths of the great mystery of God's mercy in light of our repentance. Published originally in thirteen stanzas in the 1740 collection of *Hymns and Sacred Poems*, this hymn celebrates the nature of the One "whose property always is to have mercy." Wesley demonstrates his understanding of the struggle against sin. But his hymn also reflects his confidence in the God of mercy who picks us up and sustains us in our journey toward our true home.

12 Wesley's hymn begins with deep, soul-searching questions. In the context of his Anglican tradition, through the Eucharistic liturgy of the Book of Common Prayer, he had learned to pray: "We acknowledge and bewail our manifold sins and wickedness, which we from time to time most grievously have committed, by thought, word, and deed, against thy divine majesty. We do earnestly repent, and are heartily sorry for these our misdoings; the remembrance of them is grievous to us. Have mercy upon us, have mercy upon us, most merciful Father."

13 Wesley was concerned about the way we deny Jesus, crucify him anew, profane his name, and shame him by our words and actions.

14 This stanza functions as a hinge on which the miracle of transformation turns in this hymn. It is one of the most potent statements that Charles Wesley ever penned concerning God and God's relationship to us. Our sin is strong, but God's mercy is stronger still. When we allow ourselves to fall into the embrace of the compassionate Jesus, we both know and feel God's love.

Depth of mercy! Can there be
Mercy still reserved for me!
Can my God his wrath forbear,
Me, the chief of sinners spare![12]

I my Master have denied,
I afresh have crucified,
Oft profaned his hallowed name,
Put him to an open shame.[13]

There for me the Savior stands,
Shows his wounds and spreads his hands,
God is love! I know, I feel;
Jesus weeps! But loves me still![14]

If I rightly read thy heart,
If thou all compassion art,
Bow thine ear, in mercy bow,
Pardon, and accept me now.

Pity from thine eye let fall;
By a look my soul recall,
Now the stone to flesh convert,
Cast a look, and break my heart.

Now incline me to repent,
Let me now my sins lament,
Now my foul revolt deplore,
Weep, believe, and sin no more!

CW HYMN "AFTER A RELAPSE INTO SIN" (*HSP* [1740], 82–84, STANZAS 1, 3, 9, 11–13)

15   This was Charles Wesley's favorite title for Jesus.

16   Here is a good example of the Wesleyan focus on healing and restoration as primary metaphors for salvation.

17   The key to salvation is total dependence on God, who gives us the ability to entrust our lives fully to God. Whatever God demands, God supplies.

18   True religion is heart religion. Repentance takes place primarily in the human heart. Those who focus on the self harden their hearts toward God. The singer here prays for God to break the heart so that a truly penitent spirit can emerge out of the hard shell of self-deceit.

Jesus, the Sinner's Friend

Jesu, the sinner's friend,[15] to thee
Lost and undone for aid I flee,
Weary of earth, myself, and sin—
Open thine arms, and take me in.

Pity and heal my sin-sick soul,
'Tis thou alone canst make me whole,
Fallen, till in me thine image shine,[16]
And cursed I am till thou art mine.

At last I own it cannot be
That I should fit myself for thee;
Here then to thee I all resign,
Thine is the work and only thine.[17]

CW HYMN ON GALATIANS 3:22
(*HSP* [1739], 92–93, STANZAS 1–2, 10)

O that I could repent,
  O that I could believe!
Thou by thy voice the marble rent,
  The rock in sunder cleave;
  Thou by thy two-edged sword
  My soul and spirit part,
Strike with the hammer of thy word,
  And break my stubborn heart.[18]

CW HYMN "O THAT I COULD REPENT"
(*HSP* [1749], 1:151–52, HYMN 34, STANZA 1)

✞ In a number of his hymns, Charles Wesley describes faith as "the gift unspeakable." He preached, wrote, and sang about faith. It is not too much to say that Christian faith defined his life and ministry. In his hymn on the "Author of faith," he describes the origins and nature of faith. He affirms the fact that faith is a gift. It is a source of knowledge concerning God and the way God offers salvation, hope, and healing to humanity. Like so many other great Christian teachers, he links the gift of faith to the capacity to trust God.

For Wesley, the term "faith" is also shorthand for the theological concept of justification by grace through faith. This is the door through which we pass into a vital relationship with God through Jesus. The "act of faith," that living faith *by which* we believe, is the doorway into a whole new world of hope and light. Ephesians 2:8 encapsulates Wesley's essential discovery concerning the Christian life: "for by grace you have been saved through faith; and this is not your own doing, it is the gift of God." Once we put our trust in God—once we accept God's unconditional love offered freely to us in Jesus—then we begin to love God, others, and ourselves.

1 Wesley associates faith with fire. Faith is like a quickly spreading flame, an inextinguishable blaze that sweeps through your life like a brush fire. The Holy Spirit—also linked with the image of fire—enables us to entrust our lives to God.

2 In the same way that the author of the Letter to the Hebrews defines faith as "the assurance of things hoped for, the conviction of things not seen" (11:1), Wesley understood living faith to be a sure *trust* and *confidence* in the mercy and steadfast love of God.

3 Note the way Wesley uses the central images of light and vision here. Faith enables us to see clearly.

☐ Faith

The Gift Unspeakable

Author of faith, eternal Word,
  Whose Spirit breathes the active flame,[1]
Faith, like its Finisher and Lord,
  Today as yesterday the same.

To thee our humble hearts aspire,
  And ask the gift unspeakable;
Increase in us the kindled fire,
  In us the work of faith fulfill.

By faith we know thee strong to save,
  (Save us, a present Savior thou!)
Whate'er we hope, by faith we have,
  Future and past subsisting now.[2]

Faith lends its realizing light,
  The clouds disperse, the shadows fly,
The invisible appears in sight,
  And God is seen by mortal eye.[3]

CW HYMN "THE LIFE OF FAITH" (*HSP* [1740], 6–7, STANZAS 1–3, 6)

4 Wesley alludes here to James 2:19, where the writer makes the claim that even demons believe in God. He makes the same point here as there (James 2:14–26), namely, that faith without works is dead. The faith he is talking about here is not so much a correct set of beliefs as it is a relationship of trust. This proper faith excludes no one; all can embrace it.

5 Many people think that faith refers simply to a set of beliefs to which Christians subscribe. While the term "faith" can be used in this sense as assent to certain propositions, the Wesleys emphasized faith as the foundation of a life-giving relationship that has power and energy. We might say, "I have faith in my husband, my wife, or my friend." That means we put our trust in him or her, and that relationship, built on trust, sustains us. Our relationship to God is no different.

6 John Wesley refers here to the definition of faith in Hebrews 11:1.

7 Note here the personal pronouns, reminiscent of John Wesley's account of his evangelical conversion at Aldersgate. Justification by grace through faith is a deeply personal experience. A huge chasm separates the affirmation that Jesus died for the world from the exclamation of faith, "Jesus died for *me*!" Faith does not live or save until you "own" it. But once you experience it as your own, a whole new world breaks in upon you.

8 This is a wonderful image. A bad tree cannot produce good fruit. But God can tend a tree that produces only rotten fruit and, through careful cultivation and the work of the Spirit, restore its capacity to produce good fruit that all can taste and see.

Living Faith

The faith which justifies is not purely an assent to things credible as known. It is not that speculative, notional, airy shadow which floats in the heads of some learned people. It is not a lifeless, cold, historical faith, common to devils and nominal Christians.[4] It is not learned from books or teachers. It is not a human thing, but a divine energy.[5]

CW SERMON ON ROMANS 3:23–25 (CW *SERMONS*, 201)

Trust in Christ

Faith in general is a divine, supernatural "evidence" or conviction "of things not seen," not discoverable by our bodily senses as being either past, future, or spiritual.[6] Justifying faith implies not only a divine evidence or conviction that "God was in Christ, reconciling the world unto himself," but a sure trust and confidence that Christ died for my sins, that he loved me, and gave himself for me.[7] And whenever a sinner thus believes, be it in early childhood, in the strength of years, or when old and hoary-haired, God justifies that ungodly one. God, for the sake of Christ, pardons and absolves all who have no good thing in them till then. Indeed, God had given them repentance before. But that repentance was neither more nor less than a deep sense of the want of all good and the presence of all evil. And whatever good they have or do from that hour when they first believe in God through Christ, faith does not find but bring. This is the fruit of faith. First the tree is good, and then the fruit is good also.[8]

JW SERMON "JUSTIFICATION BY FAITH" (1746), IV.2 (*WORKS*, 1:194)

✚ Many of Charles Wesley's *Redemption Hymns* focus on the central issue of faith and how the gift of faith restores fellowship with God. In this hymn, we see precisely how faith works in our lives and how God brings about new creation through this gracious gift. Throughout this hymn, Wesley celebrates two theological convictions. First, God's grace flows to all people; God excludes no one from this offer of relationship. Second, God's grace is "for me." *Because* Jesus died for *all*, he died for *me!*

9 Wesley begins the drama of redemption with God, not with us. Jesus, our friend and advocate, loved and "died for me." Despite the fact that Jesus has won our trust, entrusting our lives to him is difficult, even when the Spirit makes him known.

10 Grace initiates the process of redemption, with God reaching out to us even before we are capable of response. Our whole existence is enveloped in God's grace. Grace convicts us of our lack of faith, reveals the "smiling face" of Jesus, and calls us out of the darkness into God's marvelous light.

11 Wesley here plays with the image of light, painting masterful word pictures and drawing out the connection between redemption and creation in the biblical narrative. In creation, God sings, "Let there be light." In redemption, God commands "the light of faith to shine." The concluding couplet emphasizes the inseparable nature of God's grace in creation and redemption.

12 This is an amazing turn of phrase. The gift of faith restores our fellowship with God. If we fail to put our trust in God, we remain alienated, unhappy, and insecure in life. The wonder of God's plan of redemption is that God supplies all we need but cannot provide for ourselves. Without God, faith could never be awakened in our soul.

Father of Jesus Christ the just,
   My friend and Advocate with thee,[9]
Pity a soul who fain would trust
   In him, who loved, and died for me;
But only you can make him known,
And in my heart reveal your Son.

If drawn by your alluring grace,
   My want of living faith I feel,
Show me in Christ your smiling face;
   What flesh and blood can ne'er reveal,
Your co-eternal Son display,
And call my darkness into day.[10]

The gift unspeakable impart,
   Command the light of faith to shine,
To shine in my dark drooping heart,
   And fill me with the life divine;
Now bid the new creation be,
O God, let there be faith in me![11]

You without faith I cannot please;
   Faith without you I cannot have.[12]
But you have sent the Prince of Peace
   To seek my wandering soul, and save;
O Father! Glorify your Son,
And save me for his sake alone!

CW HYMN "FATHER OF JESUS CHRIST THE JUST"
(*REDEMPTION HYMNS* [1747], 18–19, HYMN 14, STANZAS 1–4)

13 According to Wesley, justification means pardon. God graciously forgives those who have no claim to pardon and can hardly expect it. But the crux of the problem of pardon is our acceptance of it. Paul Tillich, a great twentieth-century theologian, once said that the most difficult thing in life is to accept the fact that we are accepted. Our acceptance of the fact that God has already accepted us and loves us is the essence of the act of faith. Christ came to demonstrate this amazing love to us.

14 Those who have been justified by grace through faith experience restored fellowship with God as a deep and lasting peace. An ancient Gaelic blessing captures the essence of this experience and wishes for all the deep peace of the running wave, of the flowing air, of the quiet earth, of the shining stars, of the gentle night. The healing light of Christ pours a deep peace into our souls. The consequence of reconciliation with God is unutterable joy.

15 In his sermon "The New Birth," John Wesley provides one of his many summarizations of the way of salvation, here, in two simple points. First, God forgives us. This is something done *for* us as a consequence of Christ's redemptive work. God does for us what we cannot do for ourselves. Second, God renews us. This is something done *in* us through the restorative ministry of the Holy Spirit. Both of these movements of salvation are important. They go together and should not be separated.

16 In the Wesleyan way of salvation, justification by faith and regeneration, or new birth, are simultaneous. Faith reflects a relative change. When we put our trust in Jesus, our relationship with God changes. New birth reflects a real change. Having entrusted our lives to Jesus, the Spirit begins to change us from the inside out, helping us become more and more like Jesus.

17 Although some may find the concept of new birth somewhat difficult, probably everyone can understand the concept of a second chance. God offers us a chance to begin again in life, freeing us to start at square one.

Pardon

Justification is another word for pardon.[13] It is the forgiveness of all our sins and (what is necessarily implied therein) our acceptance with God. The price whereby this has been procured for us (commonly termed the "meritorious cause" of our justification) is the blood and righteousness of Christ, or (to express it a little more clearly) all that Christ has done and suffered for us till "he poured out his soul for the transgressors." The immediate effects of justification are the peace of God, a "peace that passeth all understanding," and a "rejoicing in hope of the glory of God," with "joy unspeakable and full of glory."[14]

JW SERMON "THE SCRIPTURE WAY OF SALVATION" (1765), I.3 (*WORKS*, 2:157–58)

New Birth

If any doctrines within the whole compass of Christianity may be properly termed fundamental they are doubtless these two—the doctrine of justification and that of the new birth.[15] The former relates to that great work which God does for us in forgiving our sins; the latter to the great work which God does in us in renewing our fallen nature. In order of time neither of these is before the other.[16] In the moment we are justified by the grace of God through the redemption that is in Jesus we are also "born of the Spirit." But in order of thinking, as it is termed, justification precedes the new birth.[17]

JW SERMON "THE NEW BIRTH" (1760), 1 (*WORKS*, 2:187)

18 In Wesley's view, the Holy Spirit functions like the midwife of the new birth. We are born again through the power of the Spirit. This spiritual regeneration parallels the process of physical birth. A long process precedes it and, just as is the case with a newborn infant, a lot of growth and development follows the moment of birth. New birth is the first step in the process of sanctification—that process by which we learn how to love God and neighbor as Jesus has loved us.

19 The use of the image of fire symbolizes the spiritual nature of the change that is taking place.

20 An "earnest" is a pledge. We still use this term in the purchase of property. If you were to buy a home, the seller would frequently require "earnest money"—a pledge of your seriousness about the transaction.

21 Wesley plays with the images of seal, stamp, and signature in this stanza. In earlier times, virtually anything of significance required an official sign that demonstrated the authentic nature of the matter at hand. We still talk about giving something the seal of our approval. The new birth is the sign of God's unfailing love, the fact that God has made us a part of the family of Jesus.

O that the Comforter would come,
   Nor visit as a transient guest,
But fix in me his constant home,
   And take possession of my breast,
And make my soul his loved abode,
The temple of indwelling God.

Come, Holy Ghost, my heart inspire,
   Attest that I am born again![18]
Come, and baptize me now with fire,[19]
   Or all your former gifts are vain.
I cannot rest in sin forgiven;
Where is the earnest of *my* heaven![20]

Where your indubitable seal
   That ascertains the kingdom mine,
The powerful stamp I long to feel,
   The signature of love divine;[21]
O shed it in my heart abroad,
Fullness of love—of heaven—of God!

CW HYMN "GROANING FOR THE SPIRIT OF ADOPTION"
(*HSP* [1740], 132, STANZAS 4–6)

✢ Charles Wesley's hymn, originally titled "Free Grace," is one of the most significant lyrical expositions of salvation in the history of Christian song. It treats both the experience and the theology of God's unconditional love and its effects on our lives in a majestic way. It identifies liberation as one of the most important themes and experiences related to redemption in Jesus. The hymn is so tightly packed that hardly a part of it can be left out.

22 This opening question shapes the whole of Wesley's theology. Today we would use the term "share" or "part" in place of Wesley's "interest." Could it possibly be, he asks, that I could have some part in this amazing and costly drama of salvation? The questions that follow amplify the extraordinary nature and the full extent of God's love for us.

23 Wesley condenses the whole doctrine of God's self-emptying in the act of Incarnation into a single line. He believes that this self-emptying is the key, in fact, to the mystery of God's love. No one is capable of understanding the depth of this mystery. All is mercy! All is gift!

24 This stanza celebrates the liberation that Jesus offers to us all. The allusions to the story of Paul and Silas in Acts 16 are unmistakable.

Liberation

And can it be that I should gain
 An interest in the Savior's blood![22]
Died he for me? who caused his pain!
 For me? who him to death pursued?
Amazing love! How can it be
That thou, my God, shouldst die for me?

He left his Father's throne above
 (So free, so infinite his grace!),
Emptied himself of all but love,[23]
 And bled for Adam's helpless race.
'Tis mercy all, immense and free!
For O my God! It found out me!

Long my imprisoned spirit lay,
 Fast bound in sin and nature's night;
Thine eye diffused a quickening ray;
 I woke, the dungeon flamed with light;
My chains fell off, my heart was free,
I rose, went forth, and followed thee.[24]

No condemnation now I dread;
 Jesus, and all in him, is mine;
Alive in him, my living Head,
 And clothed in righteousness divine,
Bold I approach the eternal throne,
And claim the crown, through Christ my own.

CW HYMN "FREE GRACE" (*HSP* [1739], 117–19, STANZAS 1, 3–4, 6)

✠ John Wesley included two sermons on Romans 8:16 in his standard collection. The question implied in this statement of St. Paul fascinated him throughout his life: "It is that very Spirit bearing witness with our spirit that we are children of God." At an early point in his life, he believed that an assurance of God's favor accompanied God's gift of faith. He insisted, in fact, that without assurance there was no valid justifying faith. If you did not *know* you were saved, in other words, you weren't. If you did not have the assurance that your sins were forgiven, they weren't. He quickly abandoned this extreme view because it simply did not reflect the experience of devout Christian people. While assurance normally accompanied the experience of conversion, it was not strictly necessary. Moreover, the "feeling" of assurance, he came to believe, cannot be made the measure of one's experience of salvation.

The Methodist claim of assurance led many in the eighteenth century to decry Wesley's followers as "enthusiasts," or religious fanatics. John defended his movement against this challenge and continued to embrace the notion of the immediate assurance of God's loving presence and forgiveness in the heart of the believer, although it was not essential to salvation. British Methodists traditionally encapsulate the way of salvation in four simple statements, one of which affirms the possibility of this kind of assurance. All people need to be saved. All people can be saved. *All people can know they are saved.* All people can be saved to the uttermost.

Assurance

The testimony of the Spirit is an inward impression on the souls of believers whereby the Spirit of God directly testifies to their spirit that they are children of God.... If we are wise, we shall be continually crying to God until the Spirit cries into our hearts, "Abba, Father!" This is the privilege of all the children of God, and without this we can never be assured that we are God's children. Without this we cannot retain a steady peace, nor avoid perplexing doubts and fears. But when we have once received this "Spirit of adoption," that peace which passes all understanding and which expels all painful doubt and fear will keep our hearts and minds in Christ Jesus.

JW SERMON "THE WITNESS OF THE SPIRIT, II" (1767), V.1, 4 (*WORKS*, 1:296, 299)

25 The two italicized words in this stanza reflect two critical concerns for Charles Wesley related to the life of faith. They can be formulated in one pressing question. How can I *know* that God loves *me*? The issues of assurance and personalization figured prominently in his effort to communicate the redeeming love of God.

26 Note the correlation in Wesley's hymn—the interface of the first and second stanzas here—between knowing and feeling. Both of these words are critical to him with regard to the experience and understanding of sin and forgiveness. Have you experienced what it means to be forgiven or to forgive? Perhaps you have offered forgiveness to someone who wounded you, or received the forgiveness of someone you have wounded with your actions or words. In that miraculous moment of exchange, you know and feel forgiveness. Hopefully, we experience this often in our human interactions. How much more important to know and feel our sins forgiven by God.

How can we sinners *know*
  Our sins on earth forgiven?
How can my Savior show
  My name inscribed in heaven?[25]
What we have felt and seen,
  With confidence we tell,
And publish to the ends of earth
  The signs infallible.

We who in Christ believe
  That he for us hath died,
We all his unknown peace receive
  And feel his blood applied.
We by his Spirit prove
  And know the things of God,
The things which freely of his love
  He hath on us bestowed.[26]

The meek and lowly heart
  That in our Savior was,
To us that Spirit doth impart
  And signs us with his cross.
Our nature's turned, our mind
  Transformed in all its powers,
And both the witnesses are joined,
  The Spirit of God with ours.

CW hymn "The Marks of Faith"
(*HSP* [1749], 2:220–22, stanzas 1, 2a, 6a, 7)

✠ In the time of the Wesleys, many Christians argued that salvation was *either* by faith *or* by works. We see the same divisions today. The effort to hold "faith alone" and "holy living" together is still a delicate balancing act. The Wesleys viewed faith as a means to love's end. The phrase "faith working by love leading to holiness of heart and life" expresses the essence of the gospel proclamation of free grace. The biblical locus for this critical theme for both Wesley brothers is Galatians 5:6: "The only thing that counts is faith working through love." Faith without activated love and works founded upon anything other than God's grace lead to equally deficient visions of the Christian life. This dynamic conception of the interrelation of faith and love, or faith and works, is one of the primary contributions of the Wesleyan theological tradition. The excerpts from both John and Charles here are classic statements of faith as a means and love as the end of true religion.

27 "Faith working by love" is the principal theme of Charles Wesley's sermon on Titus 3:8. In his exposition of this text, among the marks or effects of true faith he includes inward peace of conscience; joy; liberty, not only from the guilt but also from the power of sin; and love, for "faith works by love, and he that loveth not knoweth not God, for God is love."

28 This may be John Wesley's most eloquent testimony to the absolute centrality of love in all things. Gordon Wakefield, famed spiritual writer of the Wesleyan tradition, once remarked that Wesleyan spirituality tends to be much more Catholic than Protestant because it is oriented in the direction of love rather than faith. For some Christians, faith is the be-all and end-all. Not so for the Wesleys. Love and only love is the goal. John provides a wonderful image here of faith as the hand-maid, or servant, of love.

Faith Working by Love

Show your faith in good works. Without these, all pretensions to faith are false. These are the necessary effects or fruits or signs of a living faith. Necessary they are, not to justify us before God, but to justify us before others; or rather, not to make, but to show us acceptable; not as the cause but as the evidence of our new birth; not as conditions, but consequences and tokens of our salvation. The faith that does not work by love is an idle, barren, dead faith. It is no faith at all.[27]

CW SERMON ON 1 JOHN 3:14 (CW *SERMONS*, 150–51)

Faith itself, even Christian faith, the faith of God's elect, the faith of the operation of God, still is only the handmaid of love. As glorious and honorable as it is, it is not the end of the commandment. God has given this honor to love alone. Love is the end of all the commandments of God. Love is the end, the sole end, of every dispensation of God from the beginning of the world to the consummation of all things. And it will endure when heaven and earth flee away, for love alone never fails. Faith will totally fail. It will be swallowed up in sight in the everlasting vision of God.[28]

JW SERMON "THE LAW ESTABLISHED THROUGH FAITH, II" (1750), II.1 (*WORKS*, 2:38)

Let us join ('tis God commands)
Let us join our hearts and hands;
Help to gain our calling's hope,
Build we each the other up.

God all blessings shall dispense,
Christ shall crown his ordinance,
Meet in his appointed ways,
Nourish us with social grace.

(continued on page 143)

29 Charles Wesley's poetic reflections on Ephesians 2:8–10 provide the most memorable lyrical expression of this central theme. This hymn exhorts, urges, and encourages for all to plead for faith alone. But the purpose of this faith for which we plead is that, through it, God will form the Savior in the soul. From this foundation of faith we are called to grow into love. The indwelling Savior, the risen Jesus, shapes our personalities, characters, attitudes, and demeanor. Jesus' essence, that which he shares with the Godhead, is love—and his love becomes the very essence of our being. The hymn describes faith as an ongoing, life-transforming experience, something for which the child of God yearns and stretches forward to receive as a gift.

30 John Wesley was noted for his terse, pithy statements. In a letter related to preaching, he provides this concise rule of life.

Let us plead for faith *alone*,
Faith which by our works is shown;
God it is who justifies,
Only faith the grace *applies*;

Active faith that lives within,
Conquers hell and death and sin,
Hallows whom it first made whole,
Forms the Savior in the soul.

Let us for this faith contend,
Sure salvation is its end;
Heaven already is begun,
Everlasting life is won.

Only let us persevere
Till we see our Lord appear,
Never from the Rock remove,
Saved by faith which works by love.[29]

CW HYMN "THE LOVE FEAST, PART III"
(*HSP* [1740], 183–84, STANZAS 1, 3–4)

God loves you, therefore love and obey Christ. Christ died for you, therefore die to sin. Christ is risen, therefore rise in the image of God. Christ lives forevermore, therefore live to God till you live with God in glory. So we preached and so you believed. This is the scriptural way, the Methodist way, the true way. God grant we may never turn from this either to the right hand or to the left.[30]

JW LETTER OF DECEMBER 20, 1751 ("ON PREACHING CHRIST")
(*WORKS*, 26:488–89)

✠ Sanctification is that process by which the Spirit makes us more and more like Jesus. The word simply means "to be made holy." The Wesleys emphasized twin dimensions of sanctification: holiness of heart (internal) or love of God (a vertical dimension) and holiness of life (external) or love of neighbor (a horizontal dimension). They were not only concerned that people experience forgiveness for the brokenness in their lives (justification), but they also wanted them to move toward wholeness and healing as well (sanctification). According to the Wesleys, faith leads to love in the Christian life, and to be loving or holy is to be truly happy.

The Spirit sanctifies the believers by indwelling their lives. The glorious liberty that accompanies the Spirit not only frees us from sorrow, fear, and sin but also liberates us to love fully. In the process of sanctification there is, to use the language of the spiritual writers, an apophatic (emptying) and kataphatic (filling) rhythm. God empties us of the old and fills us with the new. The Spirit consumes, blots out, erases, and drives out our sins, emptying us of all that separates us from God; the Spirit fills us with the mind and righteousness of Jesus, restores the image of Jesus, and teaches us to love. Sanctification is a lengthy process. We do not become fully loving all at once. But it is also God's greatest gift to us as the Spirit enables us to grow into authentic children of God.

1 New birth, or regeneration, as we have seen, is the first step in the process of sanctification.

2 The essence of sanctification is spiritual renewal, to be conformed to the image of the risen Jesus.

3 Here is the apophatic/kataphatic rhythm; to have the mind of Jesus means to be emptied of all that is ungodly and to be filled with love.

☐ Holiness

The Beginning of Sanctification

And at the same time that we are justified, yes, in that very moment, sanctification begins. In that instant we are "born again," "born from above," "born of the Spirit."[1] There is a real as well as a relative change. We are inwardly renewed by the power of God.[2] We feel the "love of God shed abroad in our heart by the Holy Ghost which is given unto us," producing love to all humankind, and more especially to the children of God, expelling the love of the world, the love of pleasure, of ease, of honor, of money; together with pride, anger, self-will, and every other evil disposition—in a word, changing the "earthly, sensual, devilish" mind into "the mind which was in Christ Jesus."[3]

JW SERMON "THE SCRIPTURE WAY OF SALVATION" (1765), I.4 (WORKS, 2:158)

4 In this single-stanza hymn, Wesley reflects on a single phrase from 1 Thessalonians 4:3: "For this is the will of God, your sanctification." God's deep desire is for everyone to become loving, to be holy. We exist for this very purpose. Wesley believes that every person has a deep longing for this as well, whether they are willing to acknowledge it or not.

5 Wesley's mysticism emerges in these closing lines. God's love is a mystery into which we plunge ourselves.

6 In this hymn, originally written as a separate reflection on the story of the woman who was healed by touching the fringe of Jesus' robe (Matthew 14:36), Wesley articulates the therapeutic nature of salvation and especially the process of sanctification. The juxtaposition of these two stanzas in the creation of a new hymn demonstrates the connection between holiness and healing. God cures our disease through Jesus; God molds us into loving people.

7 If we have any hope of becoming whole, God must remove all our sin and restore our capacity to love. Perfect health means to love as God loves.

8 Growth characterizes all of life. The Wesleys believed that life in Jesus should be no different. Since the Christian religion is a relationship, why would anyone not want that relationship to grow over time? So we grow in our love of God and others in the same way that our trust in Jesus grows.

Sanctifying Grace

He wills that I should holy be;**4**
  That holiness I long to feel,
That full divine conformity
  To all my Savior's righteous will.
See, Lord, the travail of your soul
  Accomplished in the change of mine,
And plunge me, every whit made whole,
  In all the depths of love divine.**5**

CW HYMN "HE WILLS, THAT I SHOULD HOLY BE"
(SCRIPTURE HYMNS [1762], 2:325, HYMN 631 ON 1 THESSALONIANS 4:3)

Lord, I believe your power the same,
  The same your truth and grace endure,
And in your blessed hands I am,
  And trust you for a perfect cure;**6**
Come, Savior, come, and make me whole,
  Entirely all my sins remove,
To perfect health restore my soul,
  To perfect holiness and love.**7**

CW HYMN "LORD, I BELIEVE YOUR POWER THE SAME" (SCRIPTURE HYMNS [1762],
2:169–70, HYMN 171 ON MATTHEW 14:36)

Growth in Grace and Love

Love is the sum of Christian sanctification. It is the one kind of holiness which is found, only in various degrees, in the believers who are distinguished by St. John into little children, youth, and elders. The difference between one and the other properly lies in the degree of love.... In the same proportion as they grow in faith they grow in holiness.**8** They increase in love, lowliness, meekness, in every part of

(continued on page 151)

9 This is an interesting analogy. The more we love, the more consistent our love becomes in our life. Loving becomes "second nature" to us, in the same way that the beating of the heart and our breathing continue without any deviation.

10 Wesley points here to the whole purpose of our lives.

11 Charles Wesley titled this hymn "For a Tender Conscience." He understood the importance of an internal guidance mechanism—a principle within—that functions as an arbiter of words and actions.

12 Wesley knew how important the cultivation of the conscience was for the maintenance of healthy and happy relationships. Most important, he was concerned that the early Methodist people develop a biblical understanding of how good and evil forces shape decisions in our lives. Of particular concern to him was the seductive power of pride, wrong desire, and the wandering will. Permitting God to shape our lives means bringing unruly wills and passions under the control of a godly principle. It means fixing this principle at the very center of our being, the source of all words and actions. It means testing every thought, word, and deed against the measure of God's love.

the image of God, till it pleases God, after they are thoroughly convinced of inbred sin, of the total corruption of their nature, to take it all away, to purify their hearts and cleanse them from all unrighteousness ... After being filled with love, there is no more interruption of it than of the beating of their hearts.[9] And continual love bringing continual joy in the Lord, they rejoice evermore. They converse continually with the God whom they love, unto whom in everything they give thanks. And as they now love God with all their heart and with all their soul and with all their mind and with all their strength, so Jesus now reigns alone in their heart, the Lord of every motion there.[10]

JW SERMON "ON PATIENCE" (1784), 10 (*WORKS*, 3:175–76)

I want a principle within[11]
  Of watchful, godly fear,
A sensibility of sin,
  A pain to feel it near.
I want the first approach to feel
  Of pride or wrong desire,
To catch the wandering of my will,
  And quench the kindling fire.

From thee that I no more may stray,
  No more thy goodness grieve,
Grant me the filial awe, I pray,
  The tender conscience give.
Quick as the apple of an eye,
  O God, my conscience make;[12]
Awake my soul when sin is nigh,
  And keep it still awake.

CW HYMN "FOR A TENDER CONSCIENCE"
(*HSP* [1749], 2:230–31, HYMN 167, STANZAS 2–3)

⊞ Christian perfection was John Wesley's most distinctive and misunderstood teaching. With his therapeutic focus on the doctrine of salvation, it was natural for him to ask the central question, How fully can love be realized and how fully can sin be purged in this life? His distinctive answer was that there is a possibility of *entire* sanctification, or Christian perfection, *in this life*. To put it quite simply, the goal of life, he believed, is attainable in life, even if that is at the point of death. Perfection, holiness of heart and life, entire sanctification, full salvation are simply so many terms to denote one thing—loving God above all else and all else in God.

Wesley based his vision of Christian perfection on that of the early church fathers. From them, more than anything else, he learned to more precisely define perfection in terms of "perfect love." His concept of love became much more dynamic, not so much a state attained, nor something absolute, but something always improvable. In 1766 he published A *Plain Account of Christian Perfection*, arguably his most important work. The main and enduring stress of his doctrine of Christian perfection was the potential triumph of God's grace and the power of a wholehearted love of God and neighbor to displace all lesser loves and to overcome the remains of sin.

Whenever he was challenged to define precisely what he meant by Christian perfection, more often than not he simply deferred to scripture and defined it with Jesus' own words: "He said to him, 'You shall love the Lord your God with all your heart, and with all your soul, and with all your mind.' This is the greatest and first commandment. And a second is like it: 'You shall love your neighbor as yourself.' On these two commandments hang all the law and the prophets" (Matthew 22:37–39). Such love, Wesley believed, was possible in this life.

13 Wesley felt it would be difficult for any to respond to this series of rhetorical questions with anything other than a resounding "no."

Christian Perfection

By Christian perfection I mean loving God with all our heart. Do you object to this? I mean a heart and life all devoted to God. Do you desire less? I mean regaining the whole image of God. What objection to this? I mean having all the mind that was in Christ. Is this going too far? I mean walking uniformly as Christ walked. And this surely no Christian will object to.... If anyone means anything more, or anything else, by perfection, I have no concern with it.[13]

JW *JOURNAL* (QUOTING A LETTER OF JUNE 27, 1769) (*WORKS*, 22:191–92)

14 Christian perfection is nothing other than the fullest possible love of God and neighbor.

15 If Christian perfection were possible in this life, then Wesley believed it could be seen. The fruits of the Spirit bear witness to its realization of perfect love in a person's life.

16 At the Methodist Conference of 1759, Wesley made the distinction between "sin properly so called" as a voluntary transgression of a known law and "infirmities" as involuntary transgressions. As a consequence of this refined distinction, he insisted that freedom from sin is limited only to specifically voluntary violations of known laws. Christian perfection, he believed, could never be absolute, nor was he willing to define it as "sinlessness."

What is then the perfection of which people are capable while they dwell in a corruptible body? It is the complying with that kind command, "Give me thy heart." It is the "loving the Lord his God with all his heart, and with all his soul, and with all his mind." This is the sum of Christian perfection. It is all comprised in that one word, love. The first branch of it is the love of God, and as they that love God love their brothers and sisters also, it is inseparably connected with the second, "Thou shalt love thy neighbor as thyself." You shall love everyone as your own soul, as Christ loved us. "On these two commandments hang all the law and the prophets." These contain the whole of Christian perfection.[14]

St. Paul, when writing to the Galatians, places perfection in yet another view. It is the one undivided "fruit of the Spirit" which he describes thus: "The fruit of the Spirit is love, joy, peace; long-suffering, gentleness, goodness; fidelity" (so the word should be translated here), "meekness, temperance." What a glorious constellation of graces is here! Now suppose all these to be knit together in one, to be united together in the soul of a believer—this is Christian perfection.[15]

JW SERMON "ON PERFECTION" (1784), I.4, 6 (WORKS, 3:74–75)

To explain myself a little farther on this topic: 1) Not only sin properly so called (that is, a voluntary transgression of a known law), but sin improperly so called (that is, an involuntary transgression of a divine law, known or unknown) needs the atoning blood.[16] 2) I believe there is no such perfection in this life as excludes these involuntary transgressions which I apprehend to be naturally consequent [of] the ignorance and mistakes inseparable from mortality. 3) Therefore, sinless perfection is a phrase I never use, lest I should seem to contradict myself. 4) I believe a person filled with the love of God is still liable to these involuntary transgressions. 5) Such transgressions you may call sins, if you please. I do not.

JW A PLAIN ACCOUNT OF CHRISTIAN PERFECTION (1766),
19, Q. 6 (CHRISTIAN PERFECTION, 45)

17 Wesley provides this helpful summary of his views on Christian perfection near the close of *A Plain Account of Christian Perfection*.

18 You get a taste of Wesley's dry and subtle humor in this statement. The ease with which some "fell out" of perfection led him to question the authenticity of their love in the first place. Both Wesley brothers tended to be suspicious of those who made claims to this gift. On the other hand, John, in particular, never relinquished his commitment to the possibility of perfect love in this life. Charles, though, tended to conceive of perfection in the moment of death.

In the year 1764, upon a review of the whole subject, I wrote down the sum of what I had observed in the following short propositions:[17]

(1) There is such a thing as perfection, for it is again and again mentioned in Scripture.

(2) It is not so early as justification, for justified persons are to "go on unto perfection" (Hebrews 6:1).

(3) It is not so late as death, for St. Paul speaks of living men that were perfect (Philippians 3:15).

(4) It is not absolute. Absolute perfection belongs not to humans nor to angels but to God alone.

(5) It does not make a person infallible. None are infallible while they remain in the body.

(6) Is it sinless? It is not worthwhile to contend for a term. It is "salvation from sin."

(7) It is "perfect love" (1 John 4:18). This is the essence of it. Its properties, or inseparable fruits, are rejoicing evermore, praying without ceasing, and in everything giving thanks (1 Thessalonians 5:16ff).

(8) It is improvable. It is so far from lying in an indivisible point, from being incapable of increase, that those perfected in love may grow in grace far swifter than they did before.

(9) It is amissible, capable of being lost, of which we have numerous instances.[18] But we were not thoroughly convinced of this till five or six years ago.

(10) It is constantly both preceded and followed by a gradual work.

(11) But is it in itself instantaneous or not?... An instantaneous change has been wrought in some believers.... But in some this change was not instantaneous.

JW *A Plain Account of Christian Perfection* (1766),
26 (*Christian Perfection*, 106–7)

19 Both Wesleys were adamant about the believer's perpetual dependence on Jesus. No one ever grows out of the need for forgiveness or the indwelling Spirit of Jesus that makes all loves possible. The Wesleys constantly refer back to the classic Pauline text: "It is no longer I who live, but it is Christ who lives in me. And the life I now live in the flesh I live by faith in the Son of God, who loved me and gave himself for me" (Galatians 2:20).

20 Some of John Wesley's most helpful statements on perfection come from his correspondence with those who were diligently seeking to be made perfect in love. Such is the case here in his letter to a young Methodist woman.

21 One of Wesley's strongest arguments for the goal of perfect love rested in his conviction that this was a promise of God. His logic was transparent. God created us for love. As a consequence of the Fall, human beings lost their capacity to love. If God does not make the restoration of love possible in this life, then evil wins in the end. Wesley therefore links God's promise of a restored love to our very reason for being.

22 Only humility in all things has the power to conquer pride in the human spirit and make genuine love possible. Humility can only be sustained in those who put their whole trust and confidence in Jesus, the One who did not think equality with God a thing to be grasped, but emptied himself of all but love (Philippians 2:6–7).

Dependence on Christ

Christian perfection therefore does not imply (as some seem to have imagined) an exemption either from ignorance or mistake or infirmities or temptations. Indeed, it is only another term for holiness. They are two names for the same thing. Thus everyone that is perfect is holy, and everyone that is holy is, in the Scripture sense, perfect. Yet we may observe that neither in this respect is there any absolute perfection on earth. There is no "perfection of degrees," as it is termed, none which does not admit of a continual increase. Despite the level of perfection attained—how high a degree they are perfect—those perfected in love still have need to "grow in grace" and daily to advance in the knowledge and love of God their Savior.[19]

JW SERMON "CHRISTIAN PERFECTION" (1741), I.9 (*WORKS*, 2:104–5)

Thus much is certain, they that love God with all their heart and all others as themselves are scripturally perfect.[20] And surely such there are, otherwise the promise of God would be a mere mockery of human weakness.[21] Hold this fast. But then remember, on the other hand, you have this treasure in an earthen vessel.[22] You dwell in a poor, shattered house of clay which presses down the immortal spirit. Hence all your thoughts, words, and actions are so imperfect, so far from coming up to the standard (that law of love which, but for the corruptible body, you would answer in all instances), that you may well say till you go to the Christ you love:

Every moment, Lord, I need
The merit of your death.

JW LETTER OF APRIL 7, 1763, TO MISS MARCH (*LETTERS*, 4:208)

23 Here is one of John Wesley's most eloquent statements about salvation as divine therapy that heals the child of God. We are diseased and need to be healed. The goal of the process of sanctification is the fullest possible restoration to health in those who put their trust in Jesus. Wesley's concept of ultimate spiritual health is not a "perfected perfection," but a "perfecting perfection." He looked to the early church and its understanding of salvation as the restoration of the image of God for his doctrine of Christian perfection. It is essentially conformity to Jesus in all things, the believer perennially dependent on God for whatever level of restoration is made possible through the gracious power of the Holy Spirit.

24 For Wesley, pride is the root of all sin. St. Augustine argued that the primary source of our alienation from God is our desire to be like God. We want to be God, and that self-centered orientation of life destroys all avenues to love and happiness.

25 Humility, hospitality, and loving-kindness are God-shaped qualities of life. To be filled with perfect love means that these qualities flow from Jesus' holiness and righteousness in us through loving actions toward others.

Restoration—Divine Therapy

We may learn from hence, in the third place, what is the proper nature of religion, of the religion of Jesus Christ. It is ... God's method of healing a soul which is thus diseased.[23] Hereby the great Physician of souls applies medicine to heal this sickness, to restore human nature totally corrupted in all its faculties. God heals all our atheism by the knowledge of Godself and of Jesus Christ whom God has sent, by giving us faith, a divine evidence and conviction of God and of the things of God—in particular of this important truth, that Christ loved me and gave himself for me. By repentance and lowliness of heart the deadly disease of pride is healed, that of self-will by resignation, a meek and thankful submission to the will of God.[24] And for the love of the world in all its branches the love of God is the sovereign remedy. Now this is properly religion, "faith thus working by love," working the genuine, meek humility, entire deadness to the world, with a loving, thankful acquiescence in and conformity to the whole will and Word of God.

JW SERMON "ORIGINAL SIN" (1759), III.3 (WORKS, 2:184)

Father, Son, and Holy Ghost,
  In council join again
To restore thine image, lost
  By frail apostate man.
O might I thy form express,
  Through faith begotten from above,
Stamped with real holiness,
  And filled with perfect love![25]

CW HYMN (SCRIPTURE HYMNS [1762], 1:4, HYMN 5 ON GENESIS 1:3)

26 In his sermon "The Scripture Way of Salvation," Wesley provides one of his most succinct definitions of Christian perfection. He preferred to describe the goal of the Christian life as "perfect love." He used the term "perfection" because he believed it was scriptural. The term "perfect love," however, more fully describes what he is talking about. "Love" is the goal more than "perfection" is. Using the term "perfect" as a modifier of the noun "love" made more sense to him.

27 What is written on your heart? That may be a more significant question than you think. Whatever is written on our hearts reflects who we are on the deepest level. Wesley's hymn celebrates the heart of the believer—the heart upon which God has written the law of love. Originally titled "Make me a clean heart, O God" and based on Psalm 51:10, this poetic prayer represents one of his most powerful endorsements of "heart religion." Essentially, the hymn describes the nature and qualities of the heart for which he prays. But note that Wesley does not claim such a heart; rather, he realizes that "a copy" of Christ's own heart can only be given. It is God who writes on the heart, shapes the character, forms the disciple, and restores the image of Christ in the person.

Perfect Love

It is thus that we wait for entire sanctification, for a full salvation from all our sins, from pride, self-will, anger, unbelief, or, as the Apostle expresses it, "Go on to perfection." But what is perfection? The word has various senses. Here it means perfect love. It is love excluding sin, love filling the heart, taking up the whole capacity of the soul. It is love "rejoicing evermore, praying without ceasing, in everything giving thanks."[26]

JW SERMON "THE SCRIPTURE WAY OF SALVATION" (1765), I.9 (*WORKS*, 2:160)

O for a heart to praise my God,
  A heart from sin set free!
A heart that always feels thy blood,
  So freely spilt for me!

A heart in every thought renewed
  And full of love divine,
Perfect and right and pure and good,
  A copy, Lord, of thine.

Thy nature, gracious Lord, impart;
  Come quickly from above;
Write thy new name upon my heart,
  Thy new, best name of Love.[27]

CW HYMN "O FOR A HEART TO PRAISE MY GOD"
(*HSP* [1742], 30–31, HYMN ON PSALM 51, STANZAS 1, 4, 8)

28 Wesley appeals to the scriptural foundation of his view. He believes that his vision of perfect love conforms completely to the biblical witness.

29 No force in the universe is more powerful than love. Love is more powerful than hate. Love triumphs over evil. Love can conquer the disobedient heart. Love never coerces. Love never fails. Charles Wesley prayed consistently for God's love to fill his soul, and not his soul only, but the soul of every child of God. His hymn celebrates the experience of divine love and the working of the Holy Spirit—the way in which we both know and feel God in our lives. The Spirit fills our hearts with God's all-victorious love. This love is like a fire that converts, softens, melts, pierces, breaks, glows, burns, consumes, refines, illuminates, fills, and sanctifies our souls. God's all-victorious love firmly roots and fixes us in the risen Jesus. Wesley's prayer is that all might experience this in life.

Fill in this card and return it to us to be eligible for our quarterly drawing for a $100 gift certificate for SkyLight Paths books.

We hope that you will enjoy this book and find it useful in enriching your life.

Book title: _____

Your comments: _____

How you learned of this book: _____

If purchased: Bookseller _____ City _____ State _____

Please send me a free SkyLight Paths Publishing catalog. I am interested in: (check all that apply)

1. ☐ Spirituality   4. ☐ Spiritual Texts   7. ☐ Prayer/Worship
2. ☐ Mysticism/Kabbalah   5. ☐ Religious Traditions (Which ones?)   8. ☐ Meditation
3. ☐ Philosophy/Theology   6. ☐ Children's Books   9. ☐ Interfaith Resources

Name (PRINT) _____

Street _____

City _____ State _____ Zip _____

E-MAIL (FOR SPECIAL OFFERS ONLY) _____

Please send a SkyLight Paths Publishing catalog to my friend:

Name (PRINT) _____

Street _____

City _____ State _____ Zip _____

SKYLIGHT PATHS® Publishing   Tel: (802) 457-4000 • Fax: (802) 457-4004

Available at better booksellers. Visit us online at www.skylightpaths.com

Scriptural perfection is pure love filling the heart and governing all the words and actions. If your idea includes anything more, or anything else, it is not scriptural, and then no wonder that a scripturally perfect Christian does not come up to it.[28] I fear many stumble on this stumbling block. They include as many ingredients as they please—not according to Scripture, but their own imagination—in their idea of one that is perfect, and then readily deny anyone to be such who does not answer that imaginary idea. We should take more care to keep the simple scriptural account continually in our eye; pure love reigning alone in our heart and life. This is the whole of scriptural perfection.

JW *A Plain Account of Christian Perfection*, 19, Q. 25 (*Christian Perfection*, 50–51)

Jesus, thine all-victorious love
  Shed in my heart abroad;
Then shall my feet no longer rove,
  Rooted and fixed in God.

Refining fire, go through my heart,
  Illuminate my soul;
Scatter thy life through every part
  And sanctify the whole.

My steadfast soul, from falling free,
  Can now no longer move;
Jesus is all the world to me,
  And all my heart is love.[29]

CW hymn "Against Hope, Believing in Hope"
(*HSP* [1740], 157–58, stanzas 4, 9, 12)

30 The phrase "holiness of heart and life" is a simple shorthand for the fullest possible love of God and neighbor, the goal of the Christian life.

31 This John Wesley translation of a hymn by German Pietist Paul Gerhardt celebrates the central vision of the Methodists. Essentially an extended prayer, the opening two stanzas consist of two fundamental petitions. The singer pleads for love to reign without rival in the heart. So many other forces in life compete to displace love from the center of our living, but God's love is the only reality worthy to fill that space. Second, the singer pleads for total possession by love. Not only does love reign in the child of God, but the believer also yearns for love to fill his or her whole being.

Holiness of Heart and Life

By Methodists I mean a people who profess to pursue (in whatsoever measure they have attained) holiness of heart and life,[30] inward and outward conformity in all things to the revealed will of God. They place religion in a uniform resemblance of its great object, in a steady imitation of him they worship, in all Christ's imitable perfections, more particularly in justice, mercy, and truth, or universal love filling the heart and governing the life.

JW *Advice to the People called Methodists* (*Works* [Jackson], 8:352)

Jesu, thy boundless love to me
No thought can reach, no tongue declare;
O knit my thankful heart to thee
And reign without a rival there!
Thine wholly, thine alone, I am;
Be thou alone my constant flame!

O grant that nothing in my soul
May dwell, but thy pure love alone!
O may thy love possess me whole,
My joy, my treasure, and my crown;
Strange flames far from my heart remove—
My every act, word, thought, be love.[31]

JW hymn "Living by Christ," trans. Paulus Gerhardt, "O Jesu Christ, mein Schönstes Licht" (*HSP* [1739], 156–59, stanzas 1–2)

✛ This recently rediscovered text of Charles Wesley powerfully expresses the nature and consequences of perfect love restored in the child of God. Perhaps his most critical insight is that God forms our spirits through our practice of love. This final selection related to the way of salvation and its goal serves as a helpful transition into the following sections, which are related to the church and its mission. Nothing refashions our souls more than the effort—the gift—of loving those who are most unlovable. Jesus even went so far as to say that the love of our enemies demonstrates the fullest possible love in our lives. God loves like this; through the risen Lord we can love this way, too. God awakens this love in us when we permit Jesus to take full possession of our souls, when we allow the Spirit to form his character completely in our lives. Such a restoration, such a transformation, takes time, but it is God's greatest gift. To become perfect as God is perfect is to love with this kind of love. And when we do, it sparkles from within, wills that all should live, and prevails in every situation.

Come, thou holy God and true!
Come, and my whole heart renew;
Take me now, possess me whole,
Form the Savior in my soul.
In my heart thy name reveal,
Stamp me with thy Spirit's seal,
Change my nature into thine,
In me thy whole image shine.

Happy soul, whose active love
Emulates the blessed above,
In thy every action seen,
Sparkling from the soul within.
Thou to every sufferer nigh,
Hearest, not in vain, the cry
Of the widow in distress,
Of the poor and shelterless!

All God's gifts within thee move:
Tenderness, compassion, love,
Love immense, and unconfined,
Love to all of humankind.
Love, which willeth all should live,
Love, which all to all would give,
Love, that over all prevails,
Love, that never, never fails.

CW HYMN "THE BEATITUDES" (*HSP* [1749], 1:138–39,
HYMN 8, LL. 97–104, 129–36, 111–18)

PART FOUR

A Community
of Grace

✣ The experience of the gospel immediately draws us into a *community*—the church—where we can learn how to love. In the context of this new family, those who learn of Jesus receive the discipline that is necessary for them to be nourished and grow in their faith. The Wesleyan revival was an effort to recover the power of God's love inside the church.

Both Wesley brothers firmly believed that the church was always in need of rediscovering itself, of recapturing its primitive spirit. The Church of England in their day was an institution in need of repair. It had become distant from and irrelevant to the world it was called to serve. Its forms and structures had become so inflexible and devoid of life that the weight of its institutionalism was quenching the Spirit, suffocating the life of God's people. It needed a spiritual transfusion of God's power and love. In order to facilitate this renewal, the Wesleys established "little churches within the church." The early Methodist movement was a network of "societies"—neither a "church" nor a "sect." As members of a religious society, the Methodists acknowledged the truths proclaimed by the universal church and had no wish to separate from it, but claimed to cultivate an internal life of holiness, which too great an objectivity can easily neglect. Methodism was a catalyst for renewal in the church.

Several key elements constituted this movement of renewal: the rediscovery of the living Word, the rekindling of saving faith, the promotion of holistic spirituality, the development of various forms of accountable discipleship, the community's reorientation around formative worship, and the affirmation of a missional vocation as the church's primary reason for being.

1 The Wesleys drew many of their ideas and practices from the Puritan heritage of their parents. The concept of covenant dominated this tradition. In scripture, the term "covenant" refers to the sacred bond between God and God's people. In 1755, John Wesley began the practice of "covenant renewal" in his Methodist societies, using a service by Puritan pastor Richard Alleine. This "Covenant Prayer" reminds the community that we are not our own; rather, God claims us in Jesus through baptism and makes us his servants.

☐ The Character of Community

Covenant

I am no longer my own, but thine. Put me to what thou wilt, rank me with whom thou wilt. Put me to doing, put me to suffering. Let me be employed by thee or laid aside for thee, exalted for thee or brought low for thee. Let me be full, let me be empty. Let me have all things, let me have nothing. I freely and heartily yield all things to thy pleasure and disposal. And now, O glorious and blessed God, Father, Son, and Holy Spirit, thou art mine, and I am thine. So be it. And the covenant which I have made on earth, let it be ratified in heaven. Amen.[1]

COVENANT PRAYER (*UM HYMNAL*, 607)

Come, let us use the grace divine,
  And all with one accord,
In a perpetual covenant join
  Ourselves to Christ our Lord;
Give up ourselves through Jesus' power,
  His name to glorify;
And promise, in this sacred hour,
  For God to live and die.

CW HYMN "COME, LET US USE THE GRACE DIVINE" (*SCRIPTURE HYMNS* [1762], 2:36–37, HYMN 1242 ON JEREMIAH 50:5, STANZA 1)

⊞ In 1739 John Wesley published *The Nature, Design, and General Rules of Our United Societies*, the basic guide that governed the religious societies under his direction. The three simple regulations of this document—do no harm, do good, and attend upon all the ordinances of God—functioned as a Methodist rule of life. The rule could only be lived out in community and called for mutual respect, unity, and a deepening relationship with God.

2 This opening definition of the Methodist society demonstrates the importance of community in the religious life.

3 Initially, classes had an extremely practical function. John Wesley divided the community in Bristol into groups of about twelve members each in order to help pay the debt on the New Room, the first Methodist chapel. Despite its mundane beginnings, however, Wesley immediately seized upon the design as an opportunity to improve pastoral care and oversight. The classes quickly became the spiritual heartbeat of the movement. Smaller and more intimate bands provided an opportunity for intense personal introspection and rigorous mutual confession. Wesley drew up rules for these close-knit cells of four to seven members, organized for single men, married men, married women, and single women, to enhance this intimate, confessional design. It is not too much to say that early Methodism was essentially a small group movement of empowered laypeople.

4 Note the simple criterion for membership in the Methodist society.

Rule of Life

A society is no other than "a company of persons having the form and seeking the power of godliness, united in order to pray together, to receive the word of exhortation, and to watch over one another in love, that they may help each other to work out their salvation."[2]

That it may the more easily be discerned whether they are indeed working out their own salvation, each society is divided into smaller companies, called classes,[3] according to their respective places of abode....

There is only one condition previously required of those who desire admission into these societies: "a desire to flee from the wrath to come, and to be saved from their sins."[4] But wherever this is really fixed in the soul it will be shown by its fruits.

It is therefore expected of all who continue therein that they should continue to evidence their desire of salvation,

First: By doing no harm, by avoiding evil of every kind, especially that which is most generally practiced....

Secondly by doing good; by being in every kind merciful after their power; as they have opportunity, doing good of every possible sort, and, as far as possible, to all people....

Thirdly: By attending upon all the ordinances of God. These include the public worship of God, the ministry of the Word, either read or expounded, the Supper of the Lord, family and private prayer, searching the scriptures, and fasting or abstinence.

These are the General Rules of our societies, all of which we are taught of God to observe, even in the written Word which is the only rule, and the sufficient rule, both of our faith and practice. And all these we know God's Spirit writes on truly awakened hearts.

JW *The Nature, Design, and General Rules of Our United Societies* (1739)
(*Works*, 9:69–73)

✣ Two words summarize the essence of the Wesleyan way of life: accountable discipleship. Those who follow Christ watch over one another in love. They are accountable to one another in their journey of faith. The Wesleys valued the relational character of the Christian pilgrimage. No one ever stands alone; all work together to grow in love and grace.

5 John Wesley experimented with solitude at one point in his life and found it to be more of an impediment than a stimulus to his spiritual life. He drew his strength and encouragement from his relationships with other disciples of Jesus. He came to believe that Christians are made in community; there is no such thing as a solitary Christian. This is one of his strongest statements emphasizing the importance of "social religion."

Accountable Discipleship

Help us to help each other, Lord,
  Each other's cross to bear;
Let all their friendly aid afford,
  And feel each other's care.

Help us to build each other up,
  Our meager gifts improve,
Increase our faith, confirm our hope,
  And perfect us in love.

CW HYMN "PRAYER FOR PERSONS JOINED IN FELLOWSHIP, PART I"
(*HSP* [1742], 83, STANZAS 3–4)

Directly opposite to this is the gospel of Christ. Solitary religion is not to be found there. "Holy solitaries" is a phrase no more consistent with the gospel than holy adulterers. The gospel of Christ knows of no religion, but social; no holiness but social holiness.[5]

JW *HYMNS AND SACRED POEMS* (1739),
PREFACE, 5 (*WORKS* [JACKSON], 14:321)

6 | Charles Wesley provides a profoundly intimate portrait of life in the company of Jesus' followers in this hymn. Drawing close to God moves us all closer to one another. As we journey together, not only are we reconciled to God, but we experience the restoration of relationships with our companions as well. We are surrounded by companions throughout the course of the journey—the Triune God, the great cloud of witnesses or communion of saints, and our fellow pilgrims here and now.

7 | Music provides the primary metaphor for Wesley to describe the unity of the Christian community; the body of Christ is a harmonious whole.

All praise to our redeeming Lord,
  Who joins us by his grace,
And bids us, each to each restored,
  Together seek his face.
He bids us build each other up;
  And, gathered into one,
To our high calling's glorious hope
  We hand in hand go on.[6]

The gift which he on one bestows,
  We all delight to prove,
The grace through every vessel flows
  In purest streams of love.
E'en now we speak and think the same,
  And cordially agree,
Concentered all, through Jesus' name,
  In perfect harmony.[7]

CW HYMN "AT MEETING OF FRIENDS"
(REDEMPTION HYMNS [1747], 43, HYMN 32, STANZAS 1–2)

✛ The driving passion of the Wesleys was to live faithfully in Jesus and to establish communities in which others claimed this as their primary vocation as well. Two questions oriented their thinking and acting around this concern: What does it mean to live the Christian life faithfully and well? How can we help one another do so? They taught and lived a *holistic spirituality*, combining works of piety and works of mercy. On one level, this dynamic combination of Christian practices is nothing other than love of God and love of neighbor acted out in conformity to the love we see in Jesus. The dynamic connection between worship and justice, devotion and compassion, spiritual resolve and social action characterizes the active life of love. Worship and devotion (public and private acts of piety) and compassion and justice (private and public acts of mercy) define the spirituality of early Methodism. The remainder of Part Four explores works of piety, or the classic means of grace, whereas Part Five examines the Wesleyan commitment to mission in the world (works of mercy).

1 In his sermon "On Zeal," John Wesley paints this helpful word picture of the Christian life, its constitutive elements described as concentric circles revolving around the love of Jesus enthroned on the human heart. Closest to the center are the fruits of the Spirit, shaped both by acts of mercy and by acts of piety, all practiced within the context of the community of faith. You will find no better explanation or image of holistic spirituality among his many writings.

☐ A Holistic Spirituality

In a Christian believer, love sits upon the throne which is erected in the inmost soul, namely, love of God and humanity which fills the whole heart and reigns without a rival. In a circle near the throne are all holy dispositions: long-suffering, gentleness, meekness, goodness, fidelity, temperance—and if any other is comprised in "the mind which was in Christ Jesus." In an exterior circle are all the works of mercy, whether to others' souls or bodies. By these we exercise all holy dispositions; by these we continually improve them so that all these are real means of grace.... Next to these are those that are usually termed works of piety: reading and hearing the Word; public, family, private prayer; receiving the Lord's Supper; fasting or abstinence. Lastly, that the followers of Christ may the more effectually provoke one another to love, holy dispositions, and good works, our blessed Lord has united them together in one—the church, dispersed all over the earth. Every particular Christian congregation represents the universal church.[1]

JW SERMON "ON ZEAL" (1781), II.5 (*WORKS*, 3:313–14)

2 This is John Wesley's definition of the term "means of grace." The expressions "works of piety," "ordinances of God," and "means of grace" all mean the same thing. We both meet God and appropriate God's grace though these practices. The Wesleys believed that these concrete actions are essential to growth in grace. Without practicing these works there is little hope of cultivating the fruits of the Spirit in one's life. All of these are important in the quest to be like Jesus.

3 Note how Wesley also views works of mercy as means of grace. Not only do we experience God, for example, in prayer, but we also encounter God in acts of compassion and kindness. The Spirit of God conforms us to the image of Jesus in all these practices.

4 The Wesleys' spirituality is holistic in other ways as well. In this hymn a string of conjunctions describes the Christian way, which integrates head and heart, learning and piety, truth and love. You could say that whenever the head and the heart are properly united, the hands become active as well. God created us as intellectual, emotional, and volitional beings. Spiritual practices help reorient all these aspects of our being around the love of God and neighbor.

It is generally supposed that the means of grace and the ordinances of God are equivalent terms. We commonly mean by that expression what are usually termed works of piety, namely, hearing and reading the Scripture, receiving the Lord's Supper, public and private prayer, and fasting. And it is certain these are the ordinary channels which convey the grace of God to the souls of all people.[2] But are they the only means of grace? Are there no other means than these whereby God is pleased, frequently, yes, ordinarily, to convey grace to them that either love or fear God? Surely there are works of mercy as well as works of piety which are real means of grace.[3] They are more especially such to those that perform them with a single eye. And those that neglect them do not receive the grace which otherwise they might. Yes, and they lose, by a continual neglect, the grace which they had received.

JW SERMON "ON VISITING THE SICK" (1786), 1 (*WORKS*, 3:385)

Unite the pair so long disjoined
  Knowledge and vital piety,
Learning and holiness combined,
  And truth and love let us all see
In these whom up to thee we give,
Thine, wholly thine to die and live.[4]

CW HYMN "AT THE OPENING OF A SCHOOL IN KINGSWOOD"
(*HYMNS FOR CHILDREN* [1763], 35–36, STANZA 5)

✝ In a document known as the *Large Minutes*, John Wesley distinguishes between "instituted" and "prudential" means of grace. Instituted means of grace were those means either recorded in scripture or practiced by the early church. He includes prayer, Bible study, and Eucharist in his list of instituted means here, but frequently included Christian fellowship (or holy conferencing) and fasting in other lists.

Prudential means of grace, on the other hand, were distinctly Methodist disciplines that proved helpful in holy living. These practices, including the society's General Rules (discussed previously), attendance at class and band meetings, vegetarianism, and temperance of alcohol, were all acceptable additional means of living a holy life. Although not instituted in scripture, they were for Wesley nonetheless appropriate means of coming to know and follow God.

Wesley understood that our spiritual journeys are as distinctive and diverse as we are. Each one of us comes to know God in and through different means. For Wesley, the point was not which means, but how often and how seriously people devoted themselves to these practices. Although all should partake in the instituted means of grace, individuals had to choose for themselves which of the prudential means of grace helped them draw closer to God.

1 Historians of doctrine trace this classic definition of "sacrament" to St. Augustine. The Church of England defined sacraments in this way in the *39 Articles of Religion*, the historic statement of Anglican doctrine to which the Wesleys subscribed as dutiful priests.

☐ The Means of Grace

By "means of grace" I understand outward signs, words, or actions ordained by God and appointed for this end—to be the ordinary channels whereby God might convey preventing, justifying, or sanctifying grace to God's beloved children.

I use this expression, "means of grace," because I know none better and because it has been generally used in the Christian church for many ages, in particular by our own church which directs us to bless God both for the "means of grace and hope of glory" and teaches us that a sacrament is "an outward sign of inward grace, and a means whereby we receive the same."[1]

The chief of these means are prayer, whether in secret or with the great congregation; searching the Scriptures (which implies reading, hearing, and meditating thereon) and receiving the Lord's Supper, eating bread and drinking wine in remembrance of him.

JW SERMON "THE MEANS OF GRACE" (1746), II.1 (*WORKS*, 1:381)

2 Since the means of grace are precisely that, means and not ends in themselves, it is important to know how to use them properly. In his sermon "The Means of Grace," Wesley provided guidance in the proper practice of these means.

3 Wesley's first concern is to keep the means in their proper place in relation to God. Just because God promises to meet us in the means does not mean we cannot encounter God elsewhere. God is bigger than the means of grace and can use anything to draw us to Jesus. Since God has given us the means, however, we should never neglect them because they are fertile soil in which the seed of faith can grow.

4 In these several paragraphs, Wesley looks at the same issue from different perspectives. The goal toward which the means all point is communion with God. It is dangerous, therefore, to focus simply on the action itself instead of focusing on God. The actions in and of themselves have no special significance or meaning, but when connected properly to their proper goal, they are powerful tools of spiritual communion and growth in grace.

5 Beware of taking pride in any works of piety in which you engage. The very thing meant to connect us more fully with God can become an impediment if it ends up cultivating anything other than a humble, loving spirit.

6 The issue of means and ends is just as critical today as it was in the time of the Wesleys. Two problems often revolve around the connection between means and ends. First, a common attitude today is that any means can be used as long as it is for a good end. This is contrary to the gospel; means must be consistent with ends. Second, others think you can arrive at a goal without using any means to get there. This is particularly true of people who expect instant gratification. This issue relates directly to the concern Wesley identifies here.

As to the manner of using them,[2] whereon indeed it wholly depends whether they should convey any grace at all to the user, it behooves us, first, always to retain a lively sense that God is above all means.[3]Have a care therefore of limiting the Almighty.... God can convey grace either in or out of any of the means appointed. Perhaps God will....

Secondly, before you use any means let it be deeply impressed on your soul that there is no power in this. It is in itself a poor, dead, empty thing. Separate from God it is a dry leaf, a shadow....

Thirdly, in using all means, seek God alone. In and through every outward thing look singly to the power of his Spirit and the merits of God's Son....

Remember also to use all means as means, as ordained, not for their own sake, but for the purpose of renewing your soul in righteousness and true holiness. If therefore they actually tend to this, well; but if not, they are dung and dross.[4]

Lastly, after you have used any of these, take care how you value yourself thereon, how you congratulate yourself as having done some great thing. This is turning all into poison.[5]

JW SERMON "THE MEANS OF GRACE" (1746), V.4 (*WORKS*, 1:395–97)

Beware, lastly, of imagining you shall obtain the end without using the means conducive to it.[6] God can give the end without any means at all, but you have no reason to think God will. Therefore constantly and carefully use all these means which God has appointed to be the ordinary channels of God's grace. Use every means which either reason or scripture recommends as conducive (through the free love of God in Christ) either to the obtaining or increasing any of the gifts of God.

JW SERMON "THE NATURE OF ENTHUSIASM" (1750), 39 (*WORKS*, 2:59–60)

7 Wesley is absolutely clear on this point. If you do not read and study the Bible, you will not grow in spiritual wisdom. If you do not watch and pray, you will not be spiritually strong. If you do not worship God, you have little hope of being happy in life.

8 Calvinists developed a concept of unconditional election—the view that only those God chooses are saved. Wesley disagreed with this concept of election, but he did not completely abandon this biblical language. He uses the term "election" here to mean the believer's security in God's love.

9 Immersion in the means of grace cultivates faith, virtue, knowledge, temperance, patience, godliness, kindness, and love; in other words, it produces the fruits of the Spirit.

One general avenue to enthusiasm, or fanaticism, is expecting the end without the means, the expecting knowledge, for instance, without searching the Scriptures and consulting the children of God, the expecting spiritual strength without constant prayer and steady watchfulness, the expecting any blessing without hearing the Word of God at every opportunity.[7]

JW *A Plain Account of Christian Perfection*, 25,
Q. 33 (*Christian Perfection*, 89)

Keep close, I beseech you, to every means of grace. Strive to walk in all the ordinances and commandments of God blameless, giving all diligence to make your calling and election sure.[8] Add to your faith virtue, to virtue knowledge, to knowledge temperance, to temperance patience, to patience godliness, to godliness kindness, to kindness charity.[9]

JW *Journal*, April 1, 1762 (*Works*, 21:359)

✛ John and Charles Wesley were men of prayer. Virtually every day of the Wesleys' lives began and ended with Morning and Evening Prayer out of the Anglican Book of Common Prayer. But prayer did not function simply as the bookends of each day; rather, the Wesleys filled every moment of every day with the spirit of prayer. They understood that prayer provides us with glimpses of God; it enables us to find God in every aspect of our lives. Through prayer God became their constant companion in life. Like Brother Lawrence, a Carmelite devotional writer of the sixteenth century, they practiced the presence of God. According to the Wesleys, the Christian life is essentially a way of devotion, and the classics of Christian spirituality taught them the importance of total consecration in the love of God and neighbor.

The Wesleys also knew the importance of translating their vision of God in prayer into action in their daily lives. Rather than leaving us passive, true prayer moves us to act. Prayer is not about encountering an idea; it is about building a relationship with the ultimate, personal reality of the universe—the real God. Therefore, you must put on the whole of your genuine self in prayer, for as St. Augustine once observed, God does not listen to our words, because God reads our hearts. Augustine also claimed that true, whole prayer is nothing but love. Prayer is listening and speaking heart to heart and then turning that conversation into loving action. We come near to God's reign through our active love, and we need to be close to God in order to be God's agents of shalom, of peace, wholeness, justice, and well-being in the world God loves. Prayer is the key in all of this.

10 In this one stanza, Charles Wesley uses the word "pray" no fewer than six times. Could there be any question that we are to pray without ceasing?

11 Wesley uses a powerful expression here. Through our prayer we "ingrasp" all humankind. Our prayer unites us with all others and takes them all into our embrace; prayer connects us in ways that are meant to be healing and life giving.

Prayer

Pray, without ceasing pray,
  (Your Captain gives the word)
His summons cheerfully obey,
  And call upon the Lord;
  To God your every want
  In instant prayer display,
Pray always; pray, and never faint,
  Pray, without ceasing pray.[10]

In fellowship, alone,
  To God with faith draw near,
Approach God's courts, besiege God's throne
  With all the powers of prayer.
  Go to God's temple, go,
  Nor from God's altar move;
Let every house God's worship know,
  And every heart God's love.

Pour out your souls to God,
  And bow them with your knees,
And spread your hearts and hands abroad,
  And pray for Sion's peace;
  Your fellow pilgrims bear
  Forever on your mind;
Extend the arms of mighty prayer,
  Ingrasping humankind.[11]

CW HYMN "THE WHOLE ARMOR OF GOD, EPHESIANS 6"
(*HSP* [1749], 1:237–38, HYMN 258, STANZAS 12–13, 15)

12 This is a simple but profound point. God has promised to be with us in prayer; therefore, we should avail ourselves of every opportunity to be with God in these divinely appointed places of meeting. Prayer is the foundational means of grace.

13 Note here how Wesley roots his vision of prayer in scripture, in this instance in the classic texts related to prayer in the seventh chapter of St. Matthew's Gospel.

14 Charles is always confident in God's faithfulness. This is just as true of prayer as any other aspect of the Christian life. Despite our human failures and lack of faithfulness, God remains ever faithful to us.

15 We are to wait for God, not by doing nothing, but by immersing ourselves in the means of grace where God has promised to meet us.

16 In prayer we experience God—through a heart-to-heart connection—more than when we think about God.

17 Our faithfulness in prayer is based on God's prior faithfulness to us, displayed over and over again in our lives.

All who desire the grace of God are to wait for it in the way of prayer.[12] This is the express direction of our Lord himself. In his Sermon upon the Mount, after explaining at large wherein religion consists and describing the main branches of it, he adds: "Ask, and it shall be given you; seek, and ye shall find; knock, and it shall be opened unto you. For everyone that asketh, receiveth; and he that seeketh, findeth; and to him that knocketh, it shall be opened."[13]

JW SERMON "THE MEANS OF GRACE" (1746), III.1–2 (*WORKS*, 1:384–85)

Jesu, my strength, my hope,
  On you I cast my care,
With humble confidence look up,
  And know you hear my prayer.[14]

Give me on you to wait
  Till I can all things do,
On you, Almighty, to create,
  Almighty to renew.[15]

I want a heart to pray,[16]
  To pray and never cease,
Never to murmur at your stay,
  Or wish my suffering less.

This blessing above all,
  Always to pray I want,
Out of the deep on you to call,
  And never, never faint.[17]

CW HYMN "A POOR SINNER" (*HSP* [1742], 146–48, STANZAS 1, 5)

18 Here Wesley quotes Matthew 6:5 in which Jesus, as a faithful Jew, challenges the spiritual hypocrisy of contemporary religious leaders. Regardless of anyone's religious affiliation, spiritual devotion should never be used as a badge of honor or pride. Prayer, first and foremost, unites us with God.

19 No one can hide from God in prayer. The naked soul stands before God, illumined by the light of God's face. But this is no reason to fear, for the One who knows you thoroughly also loves you with an inexhaustible love.

20 John Wesley's simple definition of prayer.

21 Prayer facilitates growth in grace and love; without prayer, there is no hope of growth. Neglect of prayer kills the soul.

From works of charity or mercy our Lord proceeds to those which are termed works of piety. "And when thou prayest," he says, "thou shalt not be as the hypocrites are; for they love to pray standing in the synagogues, and in the corners of the streets, that they may be seen of men."[18] "Thou shalt not be as the hypocrites are." Hypocrisy then, or insincerity, is the first thing we are to guard against in prayer. Beware not to say what you do not mean.[19] Prayer is the lifting up of the heart to God.[20] All words of prayer without this are mere hypocrisy. Whenever therefore you attempt to pray, see that it is your one design to commune with God, to lift up your heart to God, to pour out your soul before God.

JW SERMON "UPON OUR LORD'S SERMON ON THE MOUNT, VI" (1748),
II.1 (*WORKS*, 1:575)

Perhaps no sin of omission more frequently occasions deadness of spirit than the neglect of private prayer. The lack of prayer cannot be supplied by any other ordinance whatever. Nothing can be more plain than that the life of God in the soul does not continue, much less increase, unless we use all opportunities of communing with God and pouring out our hearts before God.[21] If therefore we are negligent in this, if we suffer business, company, or any avocation whatever to prevent these secret exercises of the soul (or which comes to the same thing, to make us hurry them over in a slight and careless manner) that life will surely decay. And if we long or frequently intermit them, it will gradually die away.

JW SERMON "THE WILDERNESS STATE" (1760), II.4 (*WORKS*, 2:209)

22 Jesus provides the model for our life of prayer. He is our praying pattern. A continuous rhythm of time apart with God and constant engagement with people, dealing with the real concerns of their lives, characterized his own spirituality. He drew his energy for ministry and mission from his time of communion with God.

23 Charles Wesley draws this image from the event of the Transfiguration recorded in Luke 9. This significant event in Jesus' life reflects a pattern of contemplation and action. From his mountaintop experience he descends into the valley of life, where he is immediately confronted with a sick child whom he heals. This is the rhythm of Jesus' life throughout the Gospels—from communion with God to mission in the world. What a marvelous portrait of the life of prayer! We live out our lives as vessels, as instruments of grace, in the continual movement between the mountain and the multitude—between moments in which we glimpse the glory of God and times in which we love and give and serve for God's glory.

Holy Lamb, who thee confess,
Followers of thy holiness,
Thee they ever keep in view,
Ever ask—What shall we do?

While thou didst on earth appear,
Servant to thy servants here,
Mindful of thy place above,
All thy life was prayer and love.[22]

Early in the temple met
Let us still our Maker greet,
Nightly to the mount repair,
Join our praying pattern there.

There by wrestling faith obtain
Power to work for God again,
Power God's image to retrieve,
Power like thee our Lord to live.

Vessels, instruments of grace,
Pass we thus our happy days
'Twixt the mount and multitude,[23]
Doing or receiving good.

Glad to pray and labor on,
'Till our earthly course is run,
'Till we on the sacred tree
Bow the head and die like thee.

CW HYMN "FOR A FAMILY OF BELIEVERS"
(FAMILY HYMNS [1767], 41–42, HYMN 42, STANZAS 1, 3, 5–8)

✛ John Wesley recommended that his followers read, hear, and meditate on God's Word. He considered Spirit-led interaction with scripture to be a potent means of grace. In his sermon "The Means of Grace," he describes the centrality of the Word in the Christian life. His argument runs something like this. God richly blesses those who read and meditate on the Word. Through this means God not only gives but also confirms and increases true wisdom. If you read, study, and value the totality of God's Word, you will not wander and perish. Let all, therefore, who desire that day of salvation to dawn on their hearts, wait for it in searching the scriptures.

24 In this famous statement, John Wesley describes himself as "a man of one book." Despite the fact that few in his day were as well read as this priest, he interpreted everything in life through the lens of God's Word.

25 Wesley lays down here one of his most important principles of biblical interpretation: any part of scripture must be read in light of the whole of scripture. This hermeneutic (the technical word for one's approach to the text) safeguarded him from both proof-texting (taking any text out of context to prove a point) and misinterpretation (using one text to interpret the whole of scripture rather than the other way around).

26 Wesley had also learned the invaluable lesson of reading the Bible in community. Left to our own devices, it is easy for us to succumb to our own idiosyncratic interpretations of scripture; we may even miss the meaning or significance of a text altogether. Different perspectives on the texts of scripture guard against this problem and also enrich our understanding.

27 What Wesley means here, more than anything else, is that we must put what God reveals to us through the Word into practice in our lives.

28 Note the parallelism here between Charles's hymn and the paragraph preceding it from John Wesley's preface to his sermons. The hymn almost sounds like a lyrical paraphrase of his brother's sentiments.

Scripture

I want to know one thing, the way to heaven, how to land safe on that happy shore. God has condescended to teach the way. For this very end God came from heaven. God has written it down in a book. O give me that book! At any price, give me the book of God! I have it. Here is knowledge enough for me. Let me be *homo unius libri*.[24] Here then I am, far from the busy ways of life. I sit down alone. Only God is here. In God's presence I open, I read the book for this end, to find the way to heaven. Is there a doubt concerning the meaning of what I read? Does anything appear dark or intricate? I lift up my heart to the Father of Lights.... I then search after and consider parallel passages of scripture, "comparing spiritual things with spiritual."[25] I meditate thereon with all the attention and earnestness of which my mind is capable. If any doubt still remains, I consult those who are experienced in the things of God, and then the writings, whereby being dead, they yet speak.[26] And what I thus learn, that I teach.[27]

JW "SERMONS ON SEVERAL OCCASIONS," PREFACE, I.5 (*WORKS*, 1:104–6)

When quiet in my house I sit,
  Your book be my companion still,
My joy your sayings to repeat,
  Talk o'er the records of your will,
And search the oracles divine,
'Till every heart-felt word is mine.[28]

CW HYMN "WHEN QUIET IN MY HOUSE I SIT" (*SCRIPTURE HYMNS* [1762], 1:92–93,
HYMNS 289–92 ON DEUTERONOMY 6:7, STANZA 1)

29 The Wesleys believed that the Bible was inspired. The scriptures, as contained in the Hebrew Bible and Christian Scriptures, are the only sufficient rule for both faith and practice. In many ways, their movement of renewal was nothing other than a rediscovery of the Bible. Like most Christians, they believed that God reveals God's self to us definitively in the Word. But they also believed that the Spirit continues to inspire whoever reads and meditates on scripture today. Dead words on the page become the "living Word" for us as we engage them and seek to put them into practice in our lives.

30 Wesley lays down a significant principle here. During the sixteenth-century reformations, two primary views emerged related to scripture. 1) Some believed that a Christian ought to do only what the scriptures command. Since scripture says nothing about organs, just to illustrate, organs should not be used in worship. 2) Others argued that if scripture says nothing about a particular topic or issue, the Christian is free to accept it as long as it does not contradict the central teachings of the gospel. This group, for example, welcomed the use of organs. Wesley, perhaps obviously, embraced the latter attitude, and this opened the way for his acceptance of many practices not necessarily commanded in scripture.

The Christian rule of right and wrong is the Word of God, the writings of the Old and New Testament, all that the prophets and "holy men of old" wrote "as they were moved by the Holy Ghost." All Scripture was given by the inspiration of God and is indeed "profitable for doctrine," or teaching the whole will of God. It is helpful with regard to "reproof" of what is contrary to God's Word; "correction" of error; and "instruction (or training us up) in righteousness."[29]

This "is a lantern unto a" Christian's "feet, and a light in all his paths." Genuine Christians receive this alone as their rule of right or wrong, of whatever is really good or evil. They esteem nothing good but what is here enjoined, either directly or by plain consequence. They account nothing evil but what is here forbidden, either in terms or by undeniable inference. Whatever the Scripture neither forbids nor enjoins (either directly or by plain consequence), they believe is of an indifferent nature, in itself, neither good nor evil.[30] Scripture provides the whole and sole outward rule whereby their consciences are directed in all things.

JW SERMON "THE WITNESS OF OUR OWN SPIRIT" (1746), 6 (WORKS, 1:302–3)

31 In this hymn, Charles Wesley describes the interdependence of Word and Spirit. The Bible is like a mirror in which you can see yourself more clearly, if you truly dare to look. The Bible is much more than a recipe book or a static guide to living. It is dynamic and transforming, because the Spirit is both in it and present with us. This is where we can truly meet God! So the Spirit informs, forms, and transforms us as we read and are read by scripture.

Inspirer of the ancient seers,
  Who wrote from thee the sacred page
The same through all succeeding years,
  To us, in our degenerate age,
The Spirit of thy word impart,
And breathe the life into our heart.

While now thine oracles we read,
  With earnest prayer and strong desire,
O let thy Spirit from thee proceed,
  Our souls to waken and inspire,
Our weakness help, our darkness chase,
And guide us by the light of grace.

The secret lessons of thy grace,
  Transmitted through the word, repeat,
To train us up in all thy ways,
  To make us in thy will complete;
O lift us to the joys above,
And raise us up to perfect love.[31]

> CW HYMN "INSPIRER OF THE ANCIENT SEERS" (*SCRIPTURE HYMNS* [1762],
> 2:337–38, HYMN 664 ON 2 TIMOTHY 3:16–17, STANZAS 1, 3, 5)

✠ In the preface to his *Explanatory Notes on the Old Testament*, John Wesley prescribes a highly intentional plan for Bible study that includes daily engagement with both the Hebrew Bible and the Christian Scriptures, singleness of purpose, and practice of lessons learned. The more ancient practice of *lectio divina* (divine reading), a meditative approach to scripture developed in monastic communities, was his favored way of engaging the Bible. It could be argued that, for him, searching the scriptures was simply another form of prayer. Through a careful and prayerful exploration of the text, he was enabled to read, mark, and inwardly digest the Word of God.

Wesley's phrase "searching the scriptures" was an intentional way of defining this work of piety. He meant more than merely reading the Bible and recommended a contemplation of the text in which readers used all their faculties and senses.

32 Wesley employed another interpretive tool in his approach to scripture, namely, the analogy of faith, sometimes described as the analogy of Christ. This simply means that the Christian should read scripture through the eyes of Christ or through the interpretive lens of the way of salvation. Jesus and the way of salvation through him become the measure of all things in terms of the meaning of the Bible.

33 The resolution that concludes Wesley's prescription reflects a contemplative approach to scripture attributed to the saintly Bishop of Geneva of the previous century, Francis de Sales, and is drawn from his devotional classic, *Introduction to the Devout Life*. Salesian or Anglican meditation entails a stage of preparation to place oneself into the scene of the scripture story, a stage of consideration to relate the scene to one's own life, a stage described as affection and resolution to convert feelings into understanding and to develop a plan of action, and a conclusion to express thanksgiving to God.

If you desire to read the scriptures in such a manner as may most effectually answer this end, would it not be advisable, 1) To set apart a little time, if you can, every morning and evening for that purpose? 2) At each time, if you have leisure, to read a chapter out of the Old and one out of the New Testament; if you cannot do this, to take a single chapter or a part of one? 3) To read this with a single eye, to know the whole will of God and a fixed resolution to do it? In order to know God's will, you should, 4) Have a constant eye to the analogy of faith, the connection and harmony there is between those grand, fundamental doctrines, original sin, justification by faith, the new birth, inward and outward holiness.[32] 5) Serious and earnest prayer should be constantly used before we consult the oracles of God seeing. "Scripture can only be understood through the same Spirit whereby it was given." Our reading should likewise be closed with prayer that what we read may be written on our hearts. 6) It might also be of use, if, while we read, we were frequently to pause and examine ourselves by what we read both with regard to our hearts and lives. This would furnish us with matter of praise where we found Christ had enabled us to conform to God's blessed will and matter of humiliation and prayer where we were conscious of having fallen short. And whatever light you then receive should be used to the uttermost, and that immediately. Let there be no delay. Whatever you resolve, begin to execute the first moment you can.[33] So shall you find this word to be indeed the power of God unto present and eternal salvation.

JW EXPLANATORY NOTES ON THE OLD TESTAMENT,
PREFACE, 18 (WORKS [JACKSON], 14:253)

✠ Given the social dynamic of the early Methodist movement, it should be no surprise that Christian fellowship or conference should figure prominently among the means of grace. The Wesleys believed that whenever two or three gathered together in the name of Jesus, he was present among them. Spiritual conversation, sometimes known today as "holy conferencing," provides the support and encouragement that disciples need to grow in grace and love. The Methodist bands, classes, societies, and annual conferences all illustrate a Wesleyan commitment to community and the grace that comes through sacred fellowship. John Wesley often contrasted his own movement with others that gave little attention to this means of grace. On one occasion he went so far as to say that if someone preached like an apostle, but failed to surround those who were converted with a support system in their journey of faith, he or she was "only begetting children for the murderer." Every link in the chain of community was important to him, and time set apart simply to be together and to talk about matters of faith and practice was essential.

34 In this excerpt from *A Plain Account of the People Called Methodists*, John Wesley describes the character of the Christian fellowship experienced among his followers.

Fellowship

If it is said, "But there are some true Christians in the parish and you destroy the Christian fellowship between these and them," I answer, that which never existed cannot be destroyed. But the fellowship you speak of never existed. Therefore it cannot be destroyed. Which of those true Christians had any such fellowship with these? Who watched over them in love? Who marked their growth in grace? Who advised and exhorted them from time to time? Who prayed with them and for them as they had need? This, and this alone, is Christian fellowship. But, alas! Where is it to be found? Look east or west, north or south; name what parish you please. Is this Christian fellowship there? Rather, are not the bulk of the parishioners a mere rope of sand? What Christian connection is there between them? What intercourse in spiritual things? What watching over each other's souls? What bearing of one another's burdens? What a mere jest is it, then, to talk so gravely of destroying what never was! The real truth is just the reverse of this. We introduce Christian fellowship where it was utterly destroyed. And the fruits of it have been peace, joy, love, and zeal for every good word and work.[34]

JW *A Plain Account of the People Called Methodists* (1749),
I.11 (*Works* [Jackson], 8:251–52)

35 Charles Wesley signals the dangers inherent in the attempt to live as a Christian disciple without the support of companions in the journey. He offers a counterintuitive vision for a culture dominated by individualism and personal rights. Genuine discipleship consists in lifting up one another, carrying each other's burdens, and upholding one another in prayer. There may be echoes in Charles's hymn of the journey of the central character, Christian, in John Bunyan's classic tale, *The Pilgrim's Progress*, that great spiritual allegory depicting the believer's life and struggles.

36 The Christian pilgrim is never actually alone. The writer to the Hebrews celebrates the fact that we are all surrounded by "a great cloud of witnesses"—the fellowship or communion of saints (12:1). Those who have made the journey before us and abide now with Christ in heaven cheer on those who remain in this life. They are a perennial source of encouragement, especially as the faithful gather around the table of the Lord and share Holy Communion together.

According to the judgment of our Lord and the writings of his Apostles, it is only when we are knit together that we "have nourishment from Him, and increase with the increase of God." Neither is there any time when the weakest member can say to the strongest, or the strongest to the weakest, "I have no need of you." Accordingly, our blessed Lord, when his disciples were in their weakest state, sent them forth, not alone, but two by two.

JW *HYMNS AND SACRED POEMS* (1739),
PREFACE, 3 (*WORKS* [JACKSON], 4:320–21)

Two are better far than one
  For counsel and for fight;
How can they be warm alone,
  Or serve their God aright?**35**
Join we then our hearts and hands,
  Each to love provoke their friend,
Run the way of God's commands,
  And keep them to the end.

O that all with us might prove
  The fellowship of saints!**36**
Find supplied in Jesu's love
  What every member wants!
Gain we our high calling's prize,
  Feel our sins through Christ forgiven,
Rise, to all Christ's image, rise,
  And meet our head in heaven.

CW HYMN "TWO ARE BETTER FAR THAN ONE"
(*HSP* [1749], 2:309–10, HYMN 37, STANZAS 1, 5)

✠ John and Charles Wesley both viewed the Lord's Supper as the "chief means of grace." It is around the table of the Lord that God offers grace to all in the fullest possible expression of love divine. Charles Wesley described the Sacrament—known in different traditions as the Lord's Supper, Holy Communion, or Eucharist—as the greatest legacy that Jesus left the community of faith. While the preaching of the Word makes its appeal through the ear, the gospel is experienced in the Sacrament by way of other senses (sight, smell, taste, and touch) and with new vitality. The full, rich, and joyous Eucharistic life of early Methodism is one of the best-kept secrets of the tradition. It is a tragedy today that so few of Wesley's heirs know much, if anything, about this side of the revival.

Three essential points summarize the Wesleys' rediscovery of the importance of the Sacrament. First, God takes what is ordinary and common and fills it with divine meaning and value. Second, the Eucharist is an important social symbol, declaring the gospel to all people through a sign/act of love. Third, the actions of the Supper proclaim the gospel faithfully when words fail. As long as the church celebrates the Sacrament, there will always be a visible sign of God's love and grace in the midst of our brokenness.

Early Methodists flocked to the celebration of Holy Communion because they met God there in the person of Jesus. That is where they encountered God's love. That is where they celebrated the presence of a living Lord. That is where they received spiritual nourishment to continue their journey home. In 1745 the brothers jointly published 166 hymns in *Hymns on the Lord's Supper*, one of the most significant lyrical theologies of the Eucharist that celebrated these truths.

1 Charles alludes to several means of grace here: fasting, hearing the Word, and prayer. They are like buckets that we use to draw God's gifts out of the deep well of love and grace. In Wesley's view, however, no source of grace is more rich or meaningful than the table of the Lord.

☐ A Eucharistic Vision

The Richest Legacy

Fasting he doth and hearing bless,
  And prayer can much avail,
Good vessels all to draw the grace
  Out of salvation's well.[1]

But none like this mysterious rite
  Which dying mercy gave
Can draw forth all God's promised might
  And all God's will to save.

This is the richest legacy
  Thou hast on us bestowed,
Here chiefly, Lord, we feed on thee,
  And drink thy precious blood.

Here all thy blessings we receive,
  Here all thy gifts are given;
To those that would in thee believe,
  Pardon, and grace, and heaven.

Thus may we still in thee be blessed
  'Till all from earth remove,
And share with thee the marriage feast,
  And drink the wine above.

CW HYMN "GLORY TO HIM WHO FREELY SPENT"
(HYMNS ON THE LORD'S SUPPER [1745], 31, HYMN 42, STANZAS 2–6)

2 These two stanzas may be Charles Wesley's most eloquent tribute to the importance of the Sacrament. Note again his enumeration of the other primary means of grace. The cup of blessing that we share in the Eucharist is an unfathomable reservoir of God's grace and love.

3 In his journal, John Wesley recorded every celebration of the Sacrament in which he was involved and frequently comments on his sacramental theology. This is a particularly helpful window into his sacramental practice. Perhaps the most significant element in this reflection is the vision of God's hospitality at the table. We come because we are hungry and God feeds us. We come with our hands empty and God meets us at the very point of our need.

Chief Means of Grace

The prayer, the fast, the word conveys,
  When mixed with faith, thy life to me,
In all the channels of thy grace,
  I still have fellowship with thee,
But chiefly here my soul is fed
With fullness of immortal bread.

Communion closer far I feel,
  And deeper drink the atoning blood,
The joy is more unspeakable,
  And yields me larger draughts of God,
'Till nature faints beneath the power,
And faith filled up can hold no more.[2]

CW HYMN "WHY DID MY DYING LORD ORDAIN"
(HYMNS ON THE LORD'S SUPPER [1745], 39, HYMN 54, STANZAS 4–5)

I showed at large, 1) that the Lord's Supper was ordained by God to be a means of conveying to all either preventing or justifying or sanctifying grace according to their several necessities; 2) that the persons for whom it was ordained are all those who know and feel that they want the grace of God, either to restrain them from sin or to show their sins forgiven or to renew their souls in the image of God; 3) that inasmuch as we come to Christ's table, not to give him anything, but to receive whatsoever he sees best for us, there is no previous preparation indispensably necessary but a desire to receive whatsoever he pleases to give; and 4) that no fitness is required at the time of communicating but a sense of our state, of our utter sinfulness and helplessness.[3]

JW JOURNAL, JUNE 28, 1740 (WORKS, 19:159)

✠ Hospitality relates to the ability to make others feel comfortable and accepted. No hymn embodies this welcoming vision better than "The Great Supper." Charles Wesley first published this lengthy religious poem of twenty-four stanzas in his 1747 collection, *Redemption Hymns*. The Lord's table functions in the hymn as a paradigm of welcome, inclusion, and winsome love. God extends the invitation to all to join together at the table and desires that none be left behind. In Jesus' own table fellowship practices, those with whom he sought to eat were often the last any expected. He demonstrated his concern for the broken, the marginalized, the lonely, and the insignificant in the eyes of the world. He turned the order of the world upside down as the poor gather around his table to share in food and fellowship with him. God invites those oppressed by sin, those who wander restlessly through life, those who face emotional and physical challenges every day. God identifies with these persons and makes room for them!

4 This is a clear allusion to St. Augustine's famous statement in the opening paragraph of his *Confessions*: "You have made us for yourself, O Lord, and our hearts are restless until they rest in you."

Converting Ordinance

Come, sinners, to the gospel feast,
Let every soul be Jesus' guest,
You need not one be left behind,
For God hath bid all humankind.

Sent by my Lord, on you I call,
The invitation is to all.
Come, all the world! Come, sinner, thou!
All things in Christ are ready now.

Come, all ye souls by sin oppressed,
Ye restless wanderers after rest;[4]
Ye poor, and maimed, and halt, and blind,
In Christ a hearty welcome find.

Go then, my Lord again enjoined,
And other wandering sinners find,
Go to the hedges and highways,
And offer all my pardoning grace.

This is the time, no more delay!
This is the Lord's accepted day.
Come thou, this moment, at his call,
And live for him who died for all.

CW HYMN "THE GREAT SUPPER" (*REDEMPTION HYMNS* [1747], 63–66,
HYMN 50, STANZAS 1–2, 12, 16, 24)

5 In 1739 a debate, known as the stillness controversy, broke out in London. Several of the Moravian leaders who were part of the Fetter Lane Society argued that, since salvation is by grace alone and there is nothing anyone can do to earn it, then those who have not yet experienced conversion should do absolutely nothing. The stillness that they advocated included not going to church, not praying, not reading the Bible, and not participating in Holy Communion. John Wesley took swift action. He believed that all seekers should "wait" for God by immersing themselves in the means of grace. He encouraged them to meet Christ where Christ had promised to be.

6 This is but one instance of a narrative of conversion that took place at the Sacrament. Susanna Wesley, mother of John and Charles, actually experienced God's grace in a saving way when she received the elements of Holy Communion. The testimony of those converted at the Eucharist led the Wesleys to describe the Sacrament as a "converting ordinance." The Lord's Supper not only confirmed believers in their faith and nurtured their growth in grace, but it was also the means of bringing many people to faith. If you want to meet God, in other words, as Wesley argues here, you ought to seek God out at the table of the Lord.

In the evening I met the women of our society at Fetter Lane where some of our brethren strongly intimated that none of them had any true faith and then asserted in plain terms, 1) That till they had true faith they ought to be still, that is (as they explained themselves) to abstain from the means of grace as they are called, the Lord's Supper in particular. 2) That the ordinances are not means of grace, there being no other means than Christ....[5]

Many of those who once knew in whom they had believed were thrown into idle reasoning and thereby filled with doubts and fears from which they now found no way to escape. Many were induced to deny the gift of God and affirm they never had any faith at all, especially those who had fallen again into sin and, of consequence, into darkness. Almost all these had left off the means of grace saying they must now cease from their own works. They must now trust in Christ alone. They were poor sinners and had nothing to do but to lie at his feet.

Till Saturday, the 10th, I think I did not meet with one woman of the society who had not been upon the point of casting away her confidence in God. I then indeed found one, who, when many (according to their custom) labored to persuade her she had no faith, replied with a spirit they were not able to resist, "I know that the life which I now live, I live by faith in the Son of God, who loved me, and gave himself for me. And He has never left me one moment, since the hour He was made known to me in the breaking of bread."[6]

What is to be inferred from this undeniable matter of fact—this one who did not have faith received it at the Lord's Supper? Why, 1) That there are means of grace, that is, outward ordinances whereby the inward grace of God is ordinarily conveyed to God's children, whereby the faith that brings salvation is conveyed to them who before had it not. 2) That one of these means is the Lord's Supper. And, 3) That those who do not have this faith ought to wait for it in the use both of this and of the other means that God has ordained.

JW JOURNAL, NOVEMBER 4, 10, 1739 (WORKS, 19:119–21)

✛ The Wesleys organized their *Hymns on the Lord's Supper* into several sections that focused on the most critical aspects of their Eucharistic theology. Following the design of an earlier Anglican treatise on the Lord's Supper, Charles Wesley wrote hymns on the Sacrament as a memorial, as a sign and means of grace, and as a pledge of heaven, in addition to a concluding section on sacrifice. The first three sections closely parallel the dimensions of time. In the six lines of this one stanza, Charles alludes to all three dimensions of the meal: past, present, and future.

7 The Lord's Supper reminds us of Jesus' sacrifice for us on the cross and the supreme revelation of God's love, the past event that has shaped all time.

8 The Eucharist celebrates the presence of the living Lord and enables us to connect with Christ through faith in the here and now.

9 Holy Communion elevates our vision to God's gathering of all faithful people in the great heavenly banquet, the eternal promise that we anticipate with a living hope.

✛ The Lord's Supper is a memorial of the passion of Jesus. In it, as St. Paul says, we "proclaim the Lord's death until he comes" (1 Corinthians 11:26). This dimension of the Sacrament focuses on remembrance. We recall the sacrifice that Jesus made on the cross on our behalf. As a memorial the meal reconnects us with the love of God in the Crucified that sets us free.

In one of the most powerful hymns that Charles Wesley ever wrote, we encounter what Methodist theologian and liturgical scholar J. Ernest Rattenbury described as "a Protestant Crucifix." This hymn is a verbal, lyrical depiction of Christ on the cross. Through the power of his words and the Spirit that inspired them, Wesley draws us into the sights and sounds of that awe-full Friday afternoon.

10 The imagery of this stanza is amazing. Wesley's words make us remember something in such a way that it becomes real in the present moment.

The Dimensions of Grace

O might the sacred word
Set forth our dying Lord,
Point us to thy suffering past,[7]
  Present grace and strength impart,[8]
Give our ravished souls a taste,
  Pledge of glory in our heart.[9]

CW HYMN "O GOD OF TRUTH AND LOVE"
(HYMNS ON THE LORD'S SUPPER [1745], 38, HYMN 53, STANZA 2)

Memorial

Endless scenes of wonder rise
  With that mysterious tree,
Crucified before our eyes
  Where we our Maker see;
Jesus, Lord, what hast thou done!
  Publish we the death divine,
Stop, and gaze, and fall, and own
  Was never love like thine![10]

Never love nor sorrow was
  Like that my Jesus showed;
See him stretched on yonder cross
  And crushed beneath our load!
Now discern the deity,
  Now his heavenly birth declare!
Faith cries out 'Tis he, 'tis he,
  My God that suffers there!

CW HYMN "GOD OF UNEXAMPLED GRACE"
(HYMNS ON THE LORD'S SUPPER [1745], 16, HYMN 21, STANZAS 2–3)

☩ The Eucharist is a meal of thanksgiving. Many Christians, for various reasons, seem to have fixated on the past and have never moved into this present dimension characterized by grace and joy. Rather than a celebration, their experience of the meal is more often like that of a funeral rite. But just as "grace" and "gratitude" are closely linked words, so are grace (*charis* in Greek) and thanksgiving (in Greek, *eu-charis-tia*). In the Eucharist we celebrate God's mighty acts of salvation. But even more important, we commune with thankful, joyful hearts with a risen and present Lord by faith. The meal is a sign and means of this real presence of the risen One.

11 Wesley refers here to the resurrection account of Jesus and his journey with two of his disciples on the road to Emmaus recorded in Luke 24. His followers were not able to recognize the risen Jesus until he broke bread with them in their home.

12 As Martin Luther taught, when we gather with the faithful at the table, the Spirit opens our eyes, removes the veil, and we experience the presence of the living Jesus.

13 When we commune with the victorious Jesus, we encounter God's amazing love. We come to know that God's love is real.

Real Presence

O thou who this mysterious bread
  Didst in Emmaus break,[11]
Return, herewith our souls to feed,
  And to thy followers speak.

Unseal the volume of thy grace,
  Apply the gospel word;
Open our eyes to see thy face,
  Our hearts to know the Lord.[12]

Of thee communing still, we mourn
  Till thou the veil remove;
Talk with us, and our hearts shall burn
  With flames of fervent love.

Enkindle now the heavenly zeal,
  And make thy mercy known,
And give our pardoned souls to feel
  That God and love are one.[13]

CW HYMN "O THOU WHO THIS MYSTERIOUS BREAD"
(HYMNS ON THE LORD'S SUPPER [1745], 22–23, HYMN 29)

☩ The future dimension of Holy Communion may be the most neglected in our time. Not only is the meal a memorial and a thanksgiving celebration, but it is also a pledge of heaven and an anticipation of the consummation of all things in the love of God. It is a foretaste of that great heavenly banquet in which all the faithful will one day share. It plants the seed of hope deeply in our lives. Whenever we gather around the table, we are never alone. The "great cloud of witnesses"—those who have fought the good fight and run the race with perseverance, our heroes and mentors and loved ones in the faith—surround us and join us in one great act of praise.

14 Charles Wesley develops this image in several Eucharistic hymns. The Sacrament is simply a foretaste of the banquet that awaits us in glory.

15 These metaphors expand our vision of what happens in Holy Communion. As St. Paul wrote to the Corinthians, "What no eye has seen, nor ear heard, nor the human heart conceived, what God has prepared for those who love him" (1 Corinthians 2:9).

Pledge of Heaven

How glorious is the life above
  Which in this ordinance we *taste*;[14]
That fullness of celestial love,
  That joy which shall for ever last!

That heavenly life in Christ concealed
  These earthen vessels could not bear,
The part which now we find revealed
  No tongue of angels can declare.

The light of life eternal darts
  Into our souls a dazzling ray,
A drop of heaven o'erflows our hearts,
  And deluges the house of clay.

Sure pledge of ecstasies unknown
  Shall this divine communion be,
The ray shall rise into a sun,
  The drop shall swell into a sea.[15]

CW HYMN "HOW GLORIOUS IS THE LIFE ABOVE"
(*HYMNS ON THE LORD'S SUPPER* [1745], 87, HYMN 101)

16 Charles Wesley ponders deep questions related to the Sacrament—also described as the Holy Mystery. Notice the punctuation; sometimes question marks, sometimes exclamation points. How is Jesus present at this meal? However we answer this question, Wesley was convinced that the risen Lord was really present whenever we gather around the table, and at the meal he offers us his unfathomable grace. Wesley poses his questions in all humility and then opens his hands to receive the blessing that God desires to impart.

17 God links earth and heaven through the simple elements of wine and bread. God reveals ultimate things through common, ordinary objects. Mystery indeed!

18 Wesley uses the term "virtue" here twice. By this he means the power or the energy of Jesus. Through the Spirit, God offers us the fullness of this power in the meal, the power to love.

19 He testifies to his own certainty about the Sacrament as a means of grace. While letting the mystery remain a mystery, he declares the presence and reality of grace.

20 The ultimate expression of God's grace in the community of faith is the unity we experience around the table. In some traditions, the words of St. Paul symbolize this communion and are spoken immediately prior to the distribution of the elements: "Because there is one bread, we who are many are one body, for we all partake of the one bread" (1 Corinthians 10:17). In the Sacrament, all receive from the same loaf, all are united in one body, and all are sent out from the table for mission in God's world.

21 Charles Wesley frequently uses the terms "wonder" and "adore" in his poetry. How appropriate they are in the context of Eucharist. When all is said and done, life with God is a great mystery. At the table we encounter that mystery in an immediate and personal way. Those who experience God through Jesus around the table stop, and fall, and gaze, and own the glory of the Almighty God who is Love.

Unfathomable Grace

O the depth of love divine,
  The unfathomable grace!
Who shall say how bread and wine
  God into us conveys?
How the bread his flesh imparts,
  How the wine transmits his blood,
Fills his faithful people's hearts
  With all the life of God![16]

Let the wisest mortal show
  How we the grace receive;
Feeble elements bestow
  A power not theirs to give.[17]
Who explains the wondrous way?
  How through these the virtue came?
These the virtue did convey,[18]
  Yet still remain the same.

Sure and real is the grace,
  The manner be unknown;[19]
Only meet us in thy ways
  And perfect us in one,[20]
Let us taste the heavenly powers,
  Lord, we ask for nothing more.
Thine to bless, 'tis only ours
  To wonder and adore.[21]

CW HYMN "O THE DEPTH OF LOVE DIVINE"
(*HYMNS ON THE LORD'S SUPPER* [1745], 41, HYMN 57, STANZAS 1–2, 4)

PART FIVE

A Compassionate Mission

✢ John and Charles Wesley's rediscovery of a "mission-church paradigm" in eighteenth-century England fueled the renewal of the church. They believed that God designed the church as a redemptive community, a family that lives in and for God's vision of shalom in the world. The church draws committed Christian disciples perennially to Jesus and to one another in community (centripetal movement) and then spins them out into the world in mission and service (centrifugal movement). The Wesleys' missional practice mirrored their understanding of God— the loving Creator of all who is active and at work in the world to save and restore all creation. They developed a holistic vision of mission and evangelism that refused to separate faith and works, personal salvation and social justice, physical and spiritual needs.

1 These very familiar words of Charles Wesley declare an extremely important principle. God calls the faithful to live out discipleship in Christ as servants. God does not choose us for privilege; rather, we are called to a servant vocation, and the field of service is God's world. The children of God are to use all their gifts, all their powers, to declare the amazing love of God to all.

2 An important image from Jesus' Sermon on the Mount (Matthew 5:13–16).

3 God calls the faithful to a life in but not of the world.

4 The Wesleys root their call to Christian perfection in the concrete actions of witness, mission, and service. They orient all Christian practice to the goal of perfect love. Concrete practice of love—bearing witness to the light—leads to a fuller love of God and others.

5 Wesley mitigates here against privatization of the Christian faith. Neither private nor simplistically individualistic, faith in Jesus requires concrete, visible action in community.

☐ The Church's Calling

A charge to keep I have,
  A God to glorify,
A never-dying soul to save,
  And fit it for the sky.
  To serve the present age,
  My calling to fulfill;
O may it all my powers engage
  To do my Master's will![1]

CW HYMN "A CHARGE TO KEEP I HAVE"
(SCRIPTURE HYMNS [1762], 1:58–59, HYMN 188 ON LEVITICUS 8:35, STANZA 1)

Those of you who are Christians "are the light of the world" with regard both to your dispositions and actions.[2] Your holiness makes you as conspicuous as the sun in the midst of heaven. As you cannot go out of the world, so neither can you stay in it without appearing to all humankind.[3] You may not flee from any, and while you are among them it is impossible to hide your lowliness and meekness and those other dispositions whereby you aspire to be perfect, as your Father which is in heaven is perfect. Love cannot be hid any more than light, and least of all when it shines forth in action, when you exercise yourselves in the labor of love, in beneficence of every kind.[4]

It is as impossible to keep our religion from being seen, unless we cast it away, as it is to think of hiding the light, unless by putting it out. It is certain that a secret, unobserved religion cannot be the religion of Jesus Christ. Whatever religion can be concealed is not Christianity.[5]

JW SERMON "UPON OUR LORD'S SERMON ON THE MOUNT, IV" (1748),
II.2, 4 (WORKS, 1:539–40)

✛ This hymn of Charles Wesley elicits a profoundly missiological vision of Christian community and engagement with the dominion of God in the world. In this great Trinitarian hymn from the *Hymns on the Lord's Supper*, the disciple of Jesus asks God to claim every aspect of his or her life in a sacrifice that can only be described as covenantal. One can hear echoes of the baptismal liturgy, perhaps, in Charles's use of language. Baptism signals the beginning of discipleship, the event in which God claims each person as God's own. It also signals the commitment of the individual and the community to God's mission. In typical Wesleyan fashion, a series of "alls" characterizes the full extent of the sacrifice: all I have, all I am, all my goods, all my hours, all I know, feel, think, speak, and do. In hymns like this one, Wesley cultivates a profound vision of servant vocation, a missional conception of Christian discipleship summarized tersely in the phrase: "Claim me for thy service."

☐ An All-Consuming Sacrifice

If so low a child as I
  May to thy great glory live,
All my actions sanctify,
  All my words and thoughts receive;
Claim me for thy service, claim
All I have and all I am.

Take my soul and body's powers,
  Take my memory, mind, and will,
All my goods, and all my hours,
  All I know, and all I feel,
All I think, and speak, and do;
Take my heart—and make it new.

CW HYMN "FATHER, SON, AND HOLY GHOST" (*HYMNS ON THE LORD'S SUPPER* [1745],
129–30, HYMN 155, STANZAS 3–4)

1 In this hymn of Charles Wesley, the terms "us," "my friend," and "my beloved" have very specific reference points. He wrote this hymn for his wife on the day of their marriage. He simply bears witness to the fact that their life together would be centered in the service of others and that this service would bring them great joy. Even the galloping meter of the poetry accentuates the joyful nature of the privilege to serve.

2 The joyful service of God's children brings joy to God.

3 Not only in the context of the early Methodist societies but also in the intimacy of the home, mutual encouragement in faithfulness and service characterized the rule of life.

4 Note the string of conjunctions here. Servant ministry in the world entails both words and actions, both physical and spiritual concern, all of which Jesus modeled in his own life.

☐ Joyful Service to Others

Come, let us arise,
And press to the skies,
The summons obey,
My friend, my beloved, and hasten away![1]
  The master of all
  For our service doth call,
  And deigns to approve
With smiles of acceptance our labor of love.[2]

His burden who bear,
We alone can declare
How easy his yoke,
While to love, and good works we each other provoke.[3]
  By word and by deed,
  The bodies in need,
  The souls to relieve,
And freely as Jesus hath given to give.[4]

Then let us attend
Our heavenly friend,
In his members distressed,
With want, or affliction, or sickness oppressed;
  The prisoner relieve,
  The stranger receive,
  Supply all their wants,
And spend and be spent in assisting his saints.

CW HYMN "HYMNS FOR CHRISTIAN FRIENDS, HYMN 14"
(*HSP* [1749], 2:280–81, STANZAS 1–3)

1 Charles Wesley frequently wrote hymns to commemorate the life of a faithful Methodist who had died. The woman to whom he refers here was a leader of the Methodist Society in Bristol named Mary Naylor. In hymns such as these, Charles paints an idealized portrait of the mature Christian. It was as if he were saying, "If you want to see what a Christian perfected in love looks like, look at the life of this woman."

2 Note the emphasis Charles puts on character formation and the way the central virtues of Mary's life revolved around justice and compassion. These were shaped in her life by the practice of works of mercy.

3 This is a powerful image, particularly for a movement in which women played a crucial role.

4 Note the contrasting masculine and feminine metaphors in these two lines.

5 Charles, like his brother John, had been deeply influenced by *The Imitation of Christ* by Thomas à Kempis. The faithful Christian reflects the same characteristics we see in the life of Jesus.

☐ The Golden Rule

The golden rule she has pursued,
And did to others as she would
  Others should do to her;[1]
Justice composed her upright soul,
Justice did all her thoughts control,
  And formed her character....[2]

Affliction, poverty, disease,
Drew out her soul in soft distress,
  The wretched to relieve;
In all the works of love employed,
Her sympathizing soul enjoyed
  The blessedness to give.

A nursing mother to the poor,[3]
For them she husbanded her store,[4]
  Her life, her all, bestowed;
For them she labored day and night,
In doing good her whole delight,
  In copying after God.[5]

CW HYMN "ON THE DEATH OF MRS. MARY NAYLOR"
(CW JOURNAL, 2:338–39, 341, STANZAS PART II.3; PART III.2–3)

[6] In this sermon, John Wesley describes the authentic Christian in bold relief.

[7] The dynamic interrelation of faith and love marks the life of a genuine Christian. Following Jesus entails putting one's trust in him and then seeking to love as we have been loved by God—faith working by love leading to holiness. Faith without love can easily become dogmatic, legalistic, and judgmental; love based on anything other than radical trust in God can become sentimental, vacillating, and weak. Faith is the foundation; love is the goal.

[8] Wesley refers directly here to the so-called "golden rule" embedded in Jesus's Sermon on the Mount (Matthew 7:12). This ethic of reciprocity can be found in virtually all living religious traditions. It should be no surprise that it would figure prominently in Wesley's description of the devoted follower of Jesus.

[9] The desire to glorify God in all things defines Wesley's vision of Christian authenticity.

Who then is a Christian according to the light that God has given to this people?**6** Those who, being justified by faith, have peace with God through our Lord Jesus Christ.... Those that find the love of God shed abroad in their hearts by the Holy Ghost which is given unto them, and whom this love sweetly constrains to love their neighbors—everyone—as they love themselves.**7** Those who have learned from their Lord to be meek and lowly in heart and in every state to be content. Those who have the whole mind, all those dispositions, which were also in Christ Jesus.... Those who in their relationships do to others as they would have them do to them;**8** those who in their whole life and conversation, whether they eat or drink, or whatsoever they do, do it all to the glory of God.**9**

JW SERMON "ON GOD'S VINEYARD" (1787), I.9 (*WORKS*, 3:507–8)

1 Here is one of John Wesley's most poignant statements concerning the necessity of ministry alongside the poor. Miss March, a young convert under Wesley's preaching, had grown up in affluence and found it a particular burden to engage in ministry with the poor.

2 The doctrine of prevenient grace figured prominently in the Wesleyan way of salvation, but it also found expression in practical aspects of church life and work. In this case, the prevenient activity of God— God's leading the way and establishing a living presence before anything else is done—functions as both an impetus for action and a safeguard against pride.

3 This is a particularly powerful expression of the gospel paradox: up is down and down is up, first is last and last is first, the greatest in the kingdom of God is the servant of all.

4 There is an amazing body of hymnody related to the poor in Charles Wesley's collected works. In this particular stanza, Wesley reflects on a passage in the Acts of the Apostles (20:35–36) that reminds the Christian community of their obligation to care for the weak. It is linked with the familiar statement: "It is more blessed to give than to receive."

☐ Solidarity with the Poor

The lengthening of your life and the restoring of your health are invaluable blessings. But do you ask how you shall improve them to the glory of the Giver? And are you willing to know? Then I will tell you how. Go and see the poor and sick in their own poor little hovels. Take up your cross, woman![1] Remember the faith! Jesus went before you and will go with you.[2] Put off the gentlewoman. You bear a higher character.[3]

JW LETTER TO MISS MARCH, JUNE 9, 1775 (LETTERS, 6:153)

The poor as Jesus' bosom friends,
  The poor he makes his latest care,
To all his followers commends,
  And wills us on our hands to bear;
The poor our dearest care we make,
And love them for our Savior's sake.[4]

CW HYMN "THE POOR AS JESUS' BOSOM FRIENDS"
(MS ACTS, 421, HYMN ON ACTS 20:35–36, STANZA 1)

5   John Wesley was somewhat ahead of his time in demonstrating the intimate connection between the affluence of the few and the impoverishment of the many. He argued that the rich person's failure to give to the poor endangers his or her salvation. He insisted that for the wealthy, love of God and spiritual vitality connect directly with generosity to the poor. Wesley's vision of the moral life challenges a common assumption of many today, namely, that morality, good works, and social justice are distinct from the cultivation of a spiritual life. The life of holiness, Wesley argued, depends on one's commitment to people who are caught in structures of injustice.

6   In his preaching, Wesley could be very direct. He exhibited tremendous courage when an issue of justice or compassion captured his heart.

7   Wesley considered any persons to be rich who had enough to supply themselves and their households with the "necessaries" and "conveniences" and still have a little left over. By Wesley's estimation, therefore, many of the Methodists were, and are today, rich. He became increasingly desperate in later years to encourage these ordinary Methodists to use their prosperity wisely and generously, not only for the sake of the poor but also for their own soul's sake.

O that God would enable me once more, before I go hence and am no more seen, to lift up my voice like a trumpet to those who gain and save all they can but do not give all they can. You are the persons, some of the chief people in fact, who continually grieve the Holy Spirit of God and in a great measure stop God's gracious influence from descending on our assemblies. Many of your brothers and sisters, beloved of God, have no food to eat. They have no clothes to put on. They have no place where to lay their head. And why are they thus distressed? Because you impiously, unjustly, and cruelly detain from them what your Master and theirs lodges in your hands for the purpose of supplying their wants![5] See that poor member of Christ pinched with hunger, shivering with cold, half naked! Meantime you have plenty of this world's goods, of meat, drink, and clothing. In the name of God, what are you doing?[6] Do you neither fear God nor regard your neighbor? Why do you not share your bread with the hungry? And cover the naked with some clothes? Have you not spent on your own costly apparel what would have answered both those intentions? Did God command you to do this? Does God commend you for doing this? Did God entrust you with God's (not your) goods for this end? And does God now say, "Well done, good and faithful servant?" You well know God does not. This idle expense has no support, either from God or in your own conscience. But you say you can afford it! O be ashamed to take such miserable nonsense into your mouths. Don't ever say such a stupid thing again, such palpable absurdity! Can any steward "afford" to be an errant knave? To waste his Lord's goods? Can any servants "afford" to spend their master's money in any way other than the way in which the master appoints? So far from it that whoever does this ought to be excluded from a Christian society.[7]

JW SERMON "CAUSES OF THE INEFFICACY OF CHRISTIANITY" (1789),
9 (WORKS, 4:91–92)

1 John Wesley's sermon "On Dress," written when he was in his early eighties, contains some of his most sweeping statements against the acquisition of wealth and the neglect of the poor. He argued that it was his lifelong vocation to draw attention to the inequities in life caused by the misuse of money. The issue of wealth was a point of monumental concern for Wesley that struck at the heart of his understanding of the Christian faith. When Christians use their money properly to serve God and neighbor, then they are acting as God's faithful stewards. But when they abuse these gifts, by hoarding wealth or using it for their own luxury, they rob God as well as the poor, for whom all excess wealth is intended.

2 Note Charles Wesley's imperative tone.

3 Wesley makes it clear that the motivation for service to the poor is always love. Any foundation other than this one can lead to paternalism or resentment. His goal is always to elevate those who suffer, not to put them down. Only love can do this work.

4 Wesley concludes the hymn with this reference to Matthew 25 and the understanding, as Mother Teresa of Calcutta would say, that we find Jesus in the distressing disguise of the poor.

☐ Compassionate Action

I pray, consider this well. Perhaps you have not seen it in this light before. When you spend your money on costly clothing which you could have otherwise spared for the poor, you thereby deprive them of what God, the Proprietor of all, had lodged in your hands for their use. If so, what you put upon yourself, in effect, you are tearing from the back of the naked. The costly and delicate food which you eat you are snatching from the mouths of the hungry. For mercy, for pity, for Christ's sake, for the honor of his gospel, stay your hand. Do not throw this money away. Do not spend on nothing, yes, worse than nothing, what may clothe your poor, naked, shivering, fellow creature![1]

JW SERMON "ON DRESS" (1786), 15 (*WORKS*, 3:254)

Work for the weak, and sick, and poor,
Clothing and food for them procure,[2]
 And mindful of God's word,
Enjoy the blessedness to give,
Lay out your substance to relieve
 The members of your Lord.

Your labor which proceeds from love,[3]
Jesus shall graciously approve,
 With full felicity,
With brightest crowns your loan repay,
And tell you in that joyful day,
 "Ye did it unto Me."[4]

CW HYMN "YOUR DUTY LET THE APOSTLE SHOW"
(MS ACTS, 419, HYMN ON ACTS 20:35, STANZAS 2–3)

✢ The Wesleys challenged the injustices that they identified in their own day. Three issues in particular clamored for attention: hunger/ poverty, slavery, and war. Major demographic shifts in Britain were changing the face of the Wesleys' world as the early years of the industrial revolution ushered in an age of rapid urbanization. Huge social problems attended this shift. Starvation was rampant, particularly in the cities, and grain was often used for distilling rather than for the purpose of assuaging the hunger of the masses. By the time the Wesleys were born, African slavery had defined the Western world for a couple hundred years. Much of the wealth of the English ports was founded upon this institution. John Wesley preached against this evil, even in its vital center, the flourishing port of Bristol. Although it would go too far to describe the Wesley brothers as pacifists, they were both deeply grieved by the human toll associated with war. They spoke openly about these social evils and did all in their power to work for a more just order. It is amazing how little things have changed over the course of the centuries with regard to these very issues. Thousands die of starvation every day, human trafficking shatters innocent children, and war tears our world apart. The Wesleys would affirm that we still have much work to do in our witness to God's vision of shalom.

1 Wesley published a small tract, *Thoughts on the Present Scarcity of Provisions*, in an effort to diagnose and prescribe a solution for the problem of widespread hunger. His primary solution revolved around the use of grain in the production of bread rather than the distilling of gin.

☐ Challenging Injustice

I ask, first, why are thousands of people starving, perishing for want in every part of the nation? The fact I know. I have seen it with my eyes in every corner of the land. I have known those who could only afford to eat a little coarse food once every other day. I have known one in London (and one that a few years before had all the conveniences of life) picking up stinking fish from a dunghill and carrying them home for herself and her children. I have known another gathering the bones which the dogs had left in the streets and making broth of them to prolong a wretched life! I have heard a third artlessly declare, "Indeed I was very faint and so weak I could hardly walk, until my dog, finding nothing at home, went out and brought in a good sort of bone which I took out of his mouth and made a pure dinner!" Such is the case at this day of multitudes of people in a land flowing, as it were, with milk and honey! Abounding with all the necessaries, the conveniences, the superfluities of life![1]

JW *Thoughts on the Present Scarcity of Provisions,*
I.1 (*Works* [Jackson], 11:54)

2 John Wesley's *Thoughts upon Slavery*, published in 1774, was a clarion call to abolish both the trade and the institution of slavery in the British Empire. Here he appeals directly to those who trade in slaves that their hard hearts might be softened by the call to compassion and justice.

3 This is an excerpt from the very last letter that John Wesley ever wrote, an impassioned appeal to William Wilberforce, the famous British politician and philanthropist, to continue his parliamentary battle against the English slave trade. He likens the indefatigable abolitionist to "Athanasius against the world," a reference to an early church father who dedicated the entirety of his life to a fight against one of the early Christian heresies.

May I speak plainly to you? I must. Love constrains me; love to you, as well as to those you are concerned with. Is there a God? You know there is.... Are you a human being? Then you should have a human heart. But have you indeed? What is your heart made of? Is there no such principle as compassion there? Do you never feel another's pain? Have you no sympathy, no sense of human woe, no pity for the miserable? When you saw the flowing eyes, the heaving breasts, or the bleeding sides and tortured limbs of your fellow creatures, were you a stone, or a brute?... If your heart does relent, though in a small degree, know it is a call from the God of love. And today, if you will hear God's voice, don't harden your heart. Today resolve, God being your helper, to escape for your life.[2]

JW *Thoughts upon Slavery* (1774), V.3 (*Works* [Jackson], 11:76–77)

Unless the divine power has raised you up to be as *Athanasius contra mundum*, I do not see how you can go through your glorious enterprise in opposing that execrable villainy which is the scandal of religion, of England, and of human nature. Unless God has raised you up for this very thing, you will be worn out by the opposition of villains and devils. But if God is for you, who can be against you? Are all of them together stronger than God? O be not weary of well doing! Go on, in the name of God and in the power of God's might until even American slavery (the vilest that ever saw the sun) shall vanish away before it.[3]

JW letter to William Wilberforce, February 24, 1791 (*Letters*, 8:265)

1 In *The Doctrine of Original Sin*, John Wesley develops his most direct criticism of war. In graphic detail he depicts the scenes of war and the rationale behind war's destructive goals. Like many contemporary pacifists, he conceives war to be the sum of all sin.

2 In this hymn for peace, Charles Wesley intercedes on behalf of humanity against the "hellish rage of war." Following Christ demands that we follow the way of peace, that we turn our energies into the path of peacemaking. In the Sermon on the Mount, Jesus proclaims, "Blessed are the peacemakers, for they will be called children of God" (Matthew 5:9).

3 Wesley locates the hope for peace in the transformation of the human heart.

4 The antithesis of war is not simply the absence of fighting but the establishment of the peaceable kingdom of God. The ultimate goal in all things is perfect love—shalom.

□ Waging Peace

Who can reconcile war, I will not say to religion, but to any degree of
reason or common sense?... **1**

JW *The Doctrine of Original Sin* (1757), II.10 (*Works* [Jackson], 9:221–22)

Our earth we now lament to see
  With floods of wickedness overflowed,
With violence, wrong, and cruelty,
  One wide-extended field of blood,
Where men, like fiends, each other tear
In all the hellish rage of war.**2**

O might the universal Friend
  This havoc of his creatures see!
Bid our unnatural discord end,
  Declare us reconciled in thee!
Write kindness on our inward parts
And chase the murderer from our hearts.**3**

Who *now* against each other rise,
  The nations of the earth constrain
To follow after peace, and prize
  The blessings of thy righteous reign,
The joys of unity to prove,
The paradise of perfect love.**4**

CW hymn "For Peace" (*Intercession Hymns* [1758], 4, Hymn 2, stanzas 1, 3–4)

✠ In 1749, John Wesley published a response to the circular letter of Dr. Conyers Middleton, a Deistic spokesman and debunker of classic doctrine, in which he defended what he considered to be authentic Christianity. This tract consisted of a detailed, although sometimes quite awkward, analysis of Middleton's letter, but concluded with a section that was more of a narrative description of the genuine Christian. In 1753, Wesley decided to publish the concluding section as a separate *Account of Genuine Christianity*. Wesley devoted his entire life, in fact, to the recovery of this very thing. Then, as in our own time, many people had little idea of what an authentic Christian looked like. Today, whether distorted by misrepresentations in the media or bad examples within the ranks of the church itself, the image many people quite simply associate with Christianity is hypocrisy and judgmentalism. Tragically, Christians themselves are often the biggest obstacle to God for other people. Wesley, therefore, wanted to be very clear about authentic discipleship. He provides this portrait of the genuine Christian, filled with love and motivated by mercy and grace.

1 Note here the wide embrace of the genuine Christian. Love knows no bounds. In the same way that God's love reaches out to every human being, so the love of the authentic disciple of Jesus "ingrasps all humankind," to use the language of Charles Wesley.

2 Genuine love is not simply a feeling or an attitude. Wesley makes it clear that love must be translated into action, and that this action must be consistent with the love toward which it seeks to point.

3 This is little more than an expansion of the Wesleys' "General Rules," which include doing no harm and doing good at every opportunity.

☐ Genuine Christianity

Remembering that God is love, genuine Christians are conformed to the same likeness. They are full of love for their neighbors, of universal love, not confined to one sect or party, not restrained to those who agree with them in opinions or in outward modes of worship or to those who are allied to them by blood or recommended by nearness of place. Neither do they love those only that love them or that are endeared to them by intimacy of acquaintance. But their love resembles that of God whose mercy is over all God's works. It soars above all these scanty bounds, embracing neighbors and strangers, friends and enemies, yes, not only the good and gentle but also the disobedient, the evil and unthankful. For they love every soul that God has made, every child of humanity, of whatever place or nation....[1]

The same love is productive of all right actions.[2] It leads them into an earnest and steady discharge of all social offices, of whatever is due to relations of every kind, to their friends, to their country, and to any particular community whereof they are members. It prevents their willingly hurting or grieving any person. It guides them into a uniform practice of justice and mercy, equally extensive with the principle whence it flows. It constrains them to do all possible good, of every possible kind, to all people, and makes them invariably resolved in every circumstance of life to do that, and that only, to others which supposing they were themselves in the same situation, they would desire they should do to them.[3]

JW *A Plain Account of Genuine Christianity* (1753), I.5, 9
(*Works* [Jackson], 10:68–69)

4 Genuine love expressed by authentic Christians ought to lead to genuine reconciliation and fellowship. Elsewhere Wesley said in effect that if anyone's heart was in harmony with his heart, then he would give them his hand.

5 This must certainly be one of John Wesley's most poignant statements. His deepest desire was for love to dwell richly in the hearts of all people throughout eternity.

6 For John and Charles Wesley, God's own reconciling word is the true foundation of the abundant life, and "gratitude and benevolence" constitute a faithful response to God's offer of reconciliation. In his very last sermon, "On Faith," written in January 1791, John Wesley discusses the goal of the Christian life: gratitude to God and benevolence to all people. Benevolence or goodwill is the response of the disciple whose vision of life has been transformed by the God of love. Having discovered God's purpose for life and their place within God's unfolding story, disciples of Christ immerse themselves in and commit themselves to God's vision for a just and peace-filled world.

7 Wesley provides us with these lovely images concerning the place and role of love in our lives.

Is your heart right toward your neighbor? Do you love all humankind as yourself without exception? If you love only those that love you, what reward do you have? Do you love your enemies? Is your soul full of goodwill, of tender affection toward them? Do you love even the enemies of God? The unthankful and unholy?...

Do you show your love by your works? While you have time, as you have opportunity, do you in fact do good to all people—neighbors or strangers, friends or enemies, good or bad? Do you do them all the good you can? Endeavoring to supply all their wants, assisting them both in body and soul to the uttermost of your power? If you are thus minded, may every Christian say—yes, if you are but sincerely desirous of it, and following on till you attain—then "your heart is right, as my heart is with your heart."[4]

JW sermon "Catholic Spirit" (1750), I.17–18 (*Works*, 2:89)

Let love not visit you as a transient guest,[5] but be the constant ruling disposition of your soul. See that your heart is filled at all times and on all occasions with real, genuine benevolence,[6] not to those only that love you, but to every soul. Let it pant in your heart, let it sparkle in your eyes, let it shine on all your actions.[7] Whenever you open your lips, let it be with love, and let the law of kindness be on your tongue. Your word will then distill as the rain and as the dew upon the tender herb. Be not constrained or limited in your affection, but let it embrace every child of God. Everyone that is born of a woman has a claim to your goodwill. You owe this not to some, but to all. And let all people know that you desire both their temporal and eternal happiness as sincerely as you do your own.

JW sermon "On Pleasing All Men" (1787), II.1 (*Works*, 3:422–23)

✛ The Wesleyan vision of mission offers much to a church needing to rediscover the central place of evangelism and mission as constitutive practices of the whole people of God. Whereas evangelism includes all those activities that draw others in, mission reaches out to all, and particularly to those dear to God's heart who are most vulnerable and in need. In imitation of Jesus, a missional church woos others into the loving embrace of God and then helps them see that their mission in life, in partnership with Jesus, is to be the signposts of God's reign in this world. In this hymn, "For a preacher of the gospel," Charles Wesley reminds us of this transforming call of God and the fact that God's boundless love defines the entirety of our lives.

☐ Boundless Charity

I would the precious time redeem,
  And longer live for this alone
To spend and to be spent for them
  Who have not yet my Savior known,
Fully on these my mission prove,
And only breathe to breathe thy love.

My talents, gifts, and graces, Lord,
  Into thy blessed hands receive,
And let me live to preach thy word,
  And let me for thy glory live,
My every sacred moment spend
In publishing the sinner's friend.

Enlarge, enflame, and fill my heart
  With boundless charity divine,
So shall I all my strength exert,
  And love them with a zeal like thine,
And lead them to thine open side,
The sheep, for whom their shepherd died.

CW HYMN "FOR A PREACHER OF THE GOSPEL"
(*HSP* [1749], 1:301, HYMN 12, STANZAS 5–7)

1 In the string of rhetorical questions that follow, John Wesley holds out an olive branch—an offer of peace and reconciliation—to all others who seek to be faithful to the God of love. At the same time, these questions reveal the feelings, thoughts, and actions of the genuine Christian.

2 Wesley offers the hand of fellowship to all who seek to love as he loves. This is one of his most famous sayings.

3 What might be described as Wesley's ecumenical manifesto follows in a series of imperative "let us" statements. For those who seek the same realization of God's rule in human hearts and lives, "let us" join hearts and hands, unite, pant for God's restoration, promote scriptural Christianity, diffuse the religion of love, encourage good works, and abide in God's love.

☐ Epilogue

Are you a witness of the religion of love?[1] Are you a lover of God and all humankind? Does your heart glow with gratitude to the Giver of every good and perfect gift? The Father of the spirits of all flesh, who giveth you life, and breath, and all things? Who hath given you the Son, God's only Son, that you "might not perish, but have everlasting life"? Is your soul warm with benevolence to all people? Do you long to have all persons virtuous and happy? And does the constant tenor of your life and conversation bear witness of this? Do you "love, not in word only, but in deed and in truth"? Do you persevere in the "work of faith and the labor of love"? Do you "walk in love as Christ also loved us and gave himself for us"? Do you, as you have time, "do good unto all people"? And in as high a degree as you are able? "Whoever" thus "does the will of my Father which is in heaven, the same is my brother, and sister, and mother." Whoever you are whose heart is herein as my heart, give me your hand.[2] Come and let us magnify the Lord together, and labor to promote the kingdom of Christ upon earth.[3] Let us join hearts and hands in this blessed work, in striving to bring glory to God in the highest, by establishing peace and goodwill among all people to the uttermost of our power.... God is love and all who dwell in love dwell in God and God in them.

JW SERMON "ON LAYING THE FOUNDATION OF THE NEW CHAPEL" (1777),
II.17 (*WORKS*, 3:592)

✚ The most famous of Charles Wesley's *Redemption Hymns*, "Love divine, all loves excelling," enunciates the central themes of his and his brother's life and ministry. In Jesus he encountered the pure, unbounded love of God, a love that transcends all others and defines our lives as the children of God. The heart dominates his vision of Christianity because faith consists in relationships of love. God visits us in Jesus and offers us life abundant through the power of the Holy Spirit. The dominant theme of the Christian life is the desire never to be separated from the unconditional love we have come to know in Jesus, to serve, praise, and glory in this perfect love throughout eternity. The driving impulse of Wesley's vision of the Christian life is the fullest possible restoration of God's image in the life of every believer. The singer prays in imperative mode—visit us, reside in us, penetrate to the center of our hearts, and dwell with us forever!

4 Wesley acknowledges God as the source of pure, unbounded, extravagant love. In Jesus we see what genuine love looks like and how it behaves. Compassion defines God's life in the flesh.

5 This second line of the stanza can be read in two different ways, perhaps an intended double entendre. "Let us all" expresses the possibility of universal redemption, while "all thy life" implies God's desire to make us totally like Jesus. Those conformed to the image of Jesus in this life, claims Wesley, can be identified by their service, prayer, and praise.

6 Wesley prays for God to continue this process of restoration, moving us closer and closer to maturity in Jesus. Wesley defines this metamorphosis by the little word "till." We live in that time between what has been (what is no longer) and what will be (but is not yet). In this meantime, God continues to change us from one degree of glory to another, conforming us to the image of the risen Jesus, and sinking us deeper and deeper into love. Changed from glory into glory, the child of God falls prostrate before the Lord of all creation, "lost in wonder, love, and praise."

Love divine, all loves excelling,
  Joy of heaven, to earth come down;
Fix in us thy humble dwelling;
  All thy faithful mercies crown!
Jesus, thou art all compassion,
  Pure, unbounded love thou art;
Visit us with thy salvation;
  Enter every trembling heart.[4]

Come, Almighty to deliver,
  Let us all thy life receive;[5]
Suddenly return and never,
  Nevermore thy temples leave.
Thee we would be always blessing,
  Serve thee as thy hosts above,
Pray and praise thee without ceasing,
  Glory in thy perfect love.

Finish, then, thy new creation;[6]
  Pure and sinless let us be.
Let us see thy great salvation
  Perfectly restored in thee;
Changed from glory into glory,
  Till in heaven we take our place,
Till we cast our crowns before thee,
  Lost in wonder, love, and praise!

CW HYMN "LOVE DIVINE, ALL LOVES EXCELLING"
(REDEMPTION HYMNS [1747], 11–12, HYMN 9, STANZAS 1, 3–4)

Abbreviations ☐

Christian Perfection	*A Plain Account of Christian Perfection*. London: Epworth Press, 1952.
CW	Charles Wesley
CW *Journal*	Jackson, Thomas, ed. *The Journal of the Rev. Charles Wesley, M. A.* 2 vols. London: Mason, 1849.
CW *Sermons*	Newport, Kenneth G. C., ed. *The Sermons of Charles Wesley*. Oxford: Oxford University Press, 2001.
Family Hymns	*Hymns for the Use of Families*. Bristol: Pine, 1767.
HSP (1739)	*Hymns and Sacred Poems*. London: Strahan, 1739.
HSP (1740)	*Hymns and Sacred Poems*. London: Strahan, 1740.
HSP (1742)	*Hymns and Sacred Poems*. Bristol: Farley, 1742.
HSP (1749)	*Hymns and Sacred Poems*. 2 vols. Bristol: Farley, 1749.
Intercession Hymns	*Hymns of Intercession for all Mankind*. Bristol: Farley, 1758.
JW	John Wesley
JW *Journal*	Baker, Frank, and Richard P. Heitzenrater, eds. *The Bicentennial Edition of the Works of John Wesley*. Vols. 18–22. Nashville: Abingdon Press, 1988–1993.
KJV	King James Version
Letters	Telford, John, ed. *The Letters of the Rev. John Wesley, A. M.* 8 vols. London: Epworth Press, 1931.
MS Acts	Manuscript Poems on the Acts of the Apostles
Nativity Hymns	*Hymns for the Nativity of Our Lord*. London: Strahan, 1745.
Redemption Hymns	*Hymns for Those That Seek, and Those That Have Redemption in the Blood of Jesus Christ*. London: Strahan, 1747.

Scripture Hymns	*Short Hymns on Select Passages of the Holy Scriptures.* 2 vols. Bristol: Farley, 1762.
UM Hymnal	*The United Methodist Hymnal.* Nashville: The United Methodist Publishing House, 1989.
Whitsunday Hymns	*Hymns of Petition and Thanksgiving for the Promise of the Father.* Bristol: Farley, 1746.
Works	Baker, Frank, and Richard P. Heitzenrater, eds. *The Bicentennial Edition of the Works of John Wesley.* 35 volumes projected. Nashville: Abingdon Press, 1984–. (Volumes 7, 11, 25, and 26 originally appeared as the *Oxford Edition of the Works of John Wesley.* Oxford: Clarendon Press, 1975–83.)
Works (Jackson)	Jackson, Thomas, ed. *The Works of the Rev. John Wesley, M. A.* 3rd ed. 14 vols. London: Wesleyan Methodist Book Room, 1872.

The first edition of the hymn texts, accessed through the website of The Center for Studies in the Wesleyan Tradition, Duke Divinity School, has been used throughout in the preparation of this volume (www.divinity.duke.edu/initiatives-centers/cswt/wesley-texts).

Suggestions for Further Study ☐

Best, Gary. *Charles Wesley: A Biography*. London: Epworth Press, 2006. A masterful overview of Charles Wesley's life, time, and works.

Chilcote, Paul W. *Praying in the Wesleyan Spirit*. Nashville: Upper Room Books, 2001. An extremely useful distillation of John Wesley's standard sermons into the forms of prayer with accompanying excerpts from Charles Wesley's hymns.

———. *Recapturing the Wesleys' Vision: An Introduction to the Faith of John and Charles Wesley*. Downers Grove, IL: InterVarsity Press, 2004. One of the best introductions to the life and work of the Wesley brothers, examining their Anglican approach to Christian theology and discipleship.

Collins, Kenneth J. *John Wesley: A Theological Journey*. Nashville: Abingdon Press, 2003. One of the best theological biographies of the Methodist founder.

Kimbrough, S T, Jr., ed. *Charles Wesley: Poet and Theologian*. Nashville: Kingswood Books, 1991. A collection of essays drawn from the inaugural meeting of the Charles Wesley Society.

Kimbrough, S T, Jr. *The Lyrical Theology of Charles Wesley: A Reader*. Eugene, OR: Cascade Books, 2011. The most recent anthology of Wesley's hymns with helpful introductory essays on his lyrical theology.

Maddox, Randy L. *Responsible Grace: John Wesley's Practical Theology*. Nashville: Kingswood Books, 1994. A close, seminal study of the whole range of John Wesley's theological work.

Rack, Henry D. *Reasonable Enthusiast: John Wesley and the Rise of Methodism*. 3rd ed. London: Epworth Press, 2002. Originally published in 1993, and still the best biography of John Wesley to date, this scholarly study sets the Methodist founder and his movement against the background of his time.

Tyson, John R. *Assist Me to Proclaim: The Life and Hymns of Charles Wesley*. Grand Rapids: Wm. B. Eerdmans, 2008. An engaging study of the hymn writer by an able student of his life and ministry.

Websites

The Center for Studies in the Wesleyan Tradition of Duke Divinity School
(www.divinity.duke.edu/initiatives-centers/cswt) Contains both Wesleyan text databases and a whole range of helpful resources.

The Wesley Center Online
(http://wesley.nnu.edu) A collection of historical and scholarly resources that includes information about the Wesleyan tradition and theology as well as online texts.

Index of Texts ☐

Charles Wesley

John Wesley

Children's Spirituality

ENDORSED BY CATHOLIC, PROTESTANT, JEWISH, AND BUDDHIST RELIGIOUS LEADERS

Remembering My Grandparent: A Kid's Own Grief Workbook in the Christian Tradition *by Nechama Liss-Levinson, PhD, and Rev. Molly Phinney Baskette, MDiv* 8 x 10, 48 pp, 2-color text, HC, 978-1-59473-212-6 **$16.99** *For ages 7 & up*

Does God Ever Sleep? *by Joan Sauro, CSJ*
A charming nighttime reminder that God is always present in our lives.
10 x 8½, 32 pp, Full-color photos, Quality PB, 978-1-59473-110-5 **$8.99** *For ages 3–6*

Does God Forgive Me? *by August Gold; Full-color photos by Diane Hardy Waller*
Gently shows how God forgives all that we do if we are truly sorry.
10 x 8½, 32 pp, Full-color photos, Quality PB, 978-1-59473-142-6 **$8.99** *For ages 3–6*

God Said Amen *by Sandy Eisenberg Sasso; Full-color illus. by Avi Katz*
A warm and inspiring tale that shows us that we need only reach out to each other to find the answers to our prayers.
9 x 12, 32 pp, Full-color illus., HC, 978-1-58023-080-3 **$16.95*** *For ages 4 & up*

How Does God Listen? *by Kay Lindahl; Full-color photos by Cynthia Maloney*
How do we know when God is listening to us? Children will find the answers to these questions as they engage their senses while the story unfolds, learning how God listens in the wind, waves, clouds, hot chocolate, perfume, our tears and our laughter.
10 x 8½, 32 pp, Full-color photos, Quality PB, 978-1-59473-084-9 **$8.99** *For ages 3–6*

In God's Hands *by Lawrence Kushner and Gary Schmidt; Full-color illus. by Matthew J. Baek*
9 x 12, 32 pp, Full-color illus., HC, 978-1-58023-224-1 **$16.99*** *For ages 5 & up*

In God's Name *by Sandy Eisenberg Sasso; Full-color illus. by Phoebe Stone*
Like an ancient myth in its poetic text and vibrant illustrations, this award-winning modern fable about the search for God's name celebrates the diversity and, at the same time, the unity of all the people of the world.
9 x 12, 32 pp, Full-color illus., HC, 978-1-879045-26-2 **$16.99*** *For ages 4 & up*

Also available in Spanish: El nombre de Dios
9 x 12, 32 pp, Full-color illus., HC, 978-1-893361-63-8 **$16.95**

In Our Image: God's First Creatures
by Nancy Sohn Swartz; Full-color illus. by Melanie Hall
A playful new twist on the Genesis story—from the perspective of the animals. Celebrates the interconnectedness of nature and the harmony of all living things.
9 x 12, 32 pp, Full-color illus., HC, 978-1-879045-99-6 **$16.95*** *For ages 4 & up*

Noah's Wife: The Story of Naamah
by Sandy Eisenberg Sasso; Full-color illus. by Bethanne Andersen
Opens young readers' religious imaginations to new ideas about the well-known story of the Flood. When God tells Noah to bring the animals of the world onto the ark, God also calls on Naamah, Noah's wife, to save each plant on Earth.
9 x 12, 32 pp, Full-color illus., HC, 978-1-58023-134-3 **$16.95*** *For ages 4 & up*

Also available: Naamah: Noah's Wife (A Board Book)
by Sandy Eisenberg Sasso; Full-color illus. by Bethanne Andersen
5 x 5, 24 pp, Full-color illus., Board Book, 978-1-893361-56-0 **$7.95** *For ages 0–4*

Where Does God Live? *by August Gold and Matthew J. Perlman*
Helps children and their parents find God in the world around us with simple, practical examples children can relate to.
10 x 8½, 32 pp, Full-color photos, Quality PB, 978-1-893361-39-3 **$8.99** *For ages 3–6*

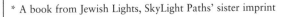

* A book from Jewish Lights, SkyLight Paths' sister imprint

Bible Stories / Folktales

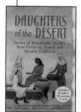

Abraham's Bind & Other Bible Tales of Trickery, Folly, Mercy and Love *by Michael J. Caduto*
New retellings of episodes in the lives of familiar biblical characters explore relevant life lessons. 6 x 9, 224 pp, HC, 978-1-59473-186-0 **$19.99**

Daughters of the Desert: Stories of Remarkable Women from Christian, Jewish and Muslim Traditions *by Claire Rudolf Murphy, Meghan Nuttall Sayres, Mary Cronk Farrell, Sarah Conover and Betsy Wharton*
Breathes new life into the old tales of our female ancestors in faith. Uses traditional scriptural passages as starting points, then with vivid detail fills in historical context and place. Chapters reveal the voices of Sarah, Hagar, Huldah, Esther, Salome, Mary Magdalene, Lydia, Khadija, Fatima and many more. Historical fiction ideal for readers of all ages.
5½ x 8¼, 192 pp, Quality PB, 978-1-59473-106-8 **$14.99** Inc. reader's discussion guide
HC, 978-1-893361-72-0 **$19.95**

The Triumph of Eve & Other Subversive Bible Tales
by Matt Biers-Ariel
These engaging retellings of familiar Bible stories are witty, often hilarious and always profound. They invite you to grapple with questions and issues that are often hidden in the original texts.
5½ x 8½, 192 pp, Quality PB, 978-1-59473-176-1 **$14.99**
Also available: **The Triumph of Eve Teacher's Guide**
8½ x 11, 44 pp, PB, 978-1-59473-152-5 **$8.99**

Wisdom in the Telling
Finding Inspiration and Grace in Traditional Folktales and Myths Retold
by Lorraine Hartin-Gelardi
6 x 9, 192 pp, HC, 978-1-59473-185-3 **$19.99**

Religious Etiquette / Reference

How to Be a Perfect Stranger, 5th Edition: The Essential Religious Etiquette Handbook *Edited by Stuart M. Matlins and Arthur J. Magida*
The indispensable guidebook to help the well-meaning guest when visiting other people's religious ceremonies. A straightforward guide to the rituals and celebrations of the major religions and denominations in the United States and Canada from the perspective of an interested guest of any other faith, based on information obtained from authorities of each religion. Belongs in every living room, library and office. Covers:
African American Methodist Churches • Assemblies of God • Bahá'í Faith • Baptist • Buddhist • Christian Church (Disciples of Christ) • Christian Science (Church of Christ, Scientist) • Churches of Christ • Episcopalian and Anglican • Hindu • Islam • Jehovah's Witnesses • Jewish • Lutheran • Mennonite/Amish • Methodist • Mormon (Church of Jesus Christ of Latter-day Saints) • Native American/First Nations • Orthodox Churches • Pentecostal Church of God • Presbyterian • Quaker (Religious Society of Friends) • Reformed Church in America/Canada • Roman Catholic • Seventh-day Adventist • Sikh • Unitarian Universalist • United Church of Canada • United Church of Christ

"The things Miss Manners forgot to tell us about religion."
—*Los Angeles Times*

"Finally, for those inclined to undertake their own spiritual journeys ... tells visitors what to expect." —*New York Times*
6 x 9, 432 pp, Quality PB, 978-1-59473-294-2 **$19.99**

The Perfect Stranger's Guide to Funerals and Grieving Practices: A Guide to Etiquette in Other People's Religious Ceremonies *Edited by Stuart M. Matlins*
6 x 9, 240 pp, Quality PB, 978-1-893361-20-1 **$16.95**

The Perfect Stranger's Guide to Wedding Ceremonies: A Guide to Etiquette in Other People's Religious Ceremonies *Edited by Stuart M. Matlins*
6 x 9, 208 pp, Quality PB, 978-1-893361-19-5 **$16.95**

Sacred Texts—SkyLight Illuminations Series

Offers today's spiritual seeker an enjoyable entry into the great classic texts of the world's spiritual traditions. Each classic is presented in an accessible translation, with facing pages of guided commentary from experts, giving you the keys you need to understand the history, context and meaning of the text.

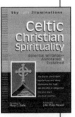

CHRISTIANITY

Celtic Christian Spirituality: Essential Writings—Annotated & Explained
Annotation by Mary C. Earle; Foreword by John Philip Newell
Explores how the writings of this lively tradition embody the gospel.
5½ x 8½, 176 pp, Quality PB, 978-1-59473-302-4 **$16.99**

The End of Days: Essential Selections from Apocalyptic Texts—
Annotated & Explained *Annotation by Robert G. Clouse, PhD*
Helps you understand the complex Christian visions of the end of the world.
5½ x 8½, 224 pp, Quality PB, 978-1-59473-170-9 **$16.99**

The Hidden Gospel of Matthew: Annotated & Explained
Translation & Annotation by Ron Miller Discover the words and events that have the strongest connection to the historical Jesus.
5½ x 8½, 272 pp, Quality PB, 978-1-59473-038-2 **$16.99**

The Infancy Gospels of Jesus: Apocryphal Tales from the Childhoods of Mary and Jesus—Annotated & Explained
Translation & Annotation by Stevan Davies; Foreword by A. Edward Siecienski, PhD
A startling presentation of the early lives of Mary, Jesus and other biblical figures that will amuse and surprise you. 5½ x 8½, 176 pp, Quality PB, 978-1-59473-258-4 **$16.99**

The Lost Sayings of Jesus: Teachings from Ancient Christian, Jewish, Gnostic and Islamic Sources—Annotated & Explained
Translation & Annotation by Andrew Phillip Smith; Foreword by Stephan A. Hoeller
This collection of more than three hundred sayings depicts Jesus as a Wisdom teacher who speaks to people of all faiths as a mystic and spiritual master.
5½ x 8½, 240 pp, Quality PB, 978-1-59473-172-3 **$16.99**

Philokalia: The Eastern Christian Spiritual Texts—Selections Annotated & Explained *Annotation by Allyne Smith; Translation by G. E. H. Palmer, Phillip Sherrard and Bishop Kallistos Ware*
The first approachable introduction to the wisdom of the Philokalia, the classic text of Eastern Christian spirituality. 5½ x 8½, 240 pp, Quality PB, 978-1-59473-103-7 **$16.99**

The Sacred Writings of Paul: Selections Annotated & Explained
Translation & Annotation by Ron Miller Leads you into the exciting immediacy of Paul's teachings. 5½ x 8½, 224 pp, Quality PB, 978-1-59473-213-3 **$16.99**

Saint Augustine of Hippo: Selections from *Confessions* and Other Essential Writings—Annotated & Explained
Annotation by Joseph T. Kelley, PhD; Translation by the Augustinian Heritage Institute
Provides insight into the mind and heart of this foundational Christian figure.
5½ x 8½, 272 pp, Quality PB, 978-1-59473-282-9 **$16.99**

St. Ignatius Loyola—The Spiritual Writings: Selections Annotated & Explained *Annotation by Mark Mossa, SJ*
Draws from contemporary translations of original texts focusing on the practical mysticism of Ignatius of Loyola. 5½ x 8½, 224 pp (est), Quality PB, 978-1-59473-301-7 **$16.99**

Sex Texts from the Bible: Selections Annotated & Explained
Translation & Annotation by Teresa J. Hornsby; Foreword by Amy-Jill Levine
Demystifies the Bible's ideas on gender roles, marriage, sexual orientation, virginity, lust and sexual pleasure. 5½ x 8½, 208 pp, Quality PB, 978-1-59473-217-1 **$16.99**

Sacred Texts—continued

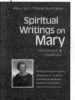

CHRISTIANITY—continued

Spiritual Writings on Mary: Annotated & Explained
Annotation by Mary Ford-Grabowsky; Foreword by Andrew Harvey
Examines the role of Mary, the mother of Jesus, as a source of inspiration in
history and in life today. 5½ x 8½, 288 pp, Quality PB, 978-1-59473-001-6 **$16.99**

The Way of a Pilgrim: The Jesus Prayer Journey—Annotated & Explained
Translation & Annotation by Gleb Pokrovsky; Foreword by Andrew Harvey
A classic of Russian Orthodox spirituality.
5½ x 8½, 160 pp, Illus., Quality PB, 978-1-893361-31-7 **$14.95**

GNOSTICISM

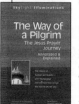

Gnostic Writings on the Soul: Annotated & Explained
Translation & Annotation by Andrew Phillip Smith; Foreword by Stephan A. Hoeller
Reveals the inspiring ways your soul can remember and return to its unique,
divine purpose. 5½ x 8½, 144 pp, Quality PB, 978-1-59473-220-1 **$16.99**

The Gospel of Philip: Annotated & Explained
Translation & Annotation by Andrew Phillip Smith; Foreword by Stevan Davies
Reveals otherwise unrecorded sayings of Jesus and fragments of Gnostic mythology.
5½ x 8½, 160 pp, Quality PB, 978-1-59473-111-2 **$16.99**

The Gospel of Thomas: Annotated & Explained
Translation & Annotation by Stevan Davies; Foreword by Andrew Harvey
Sheds new light on the origins of Christianity and portrays Jesus as a wisdom-loving sage.
5½ x 8½, 192 pp, Quality PB, 978-1-893361-45-4 **$16.99**

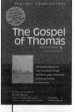

The Secret Book of John: The Gnostic Gospel—Annotated & Explained
Translation & Annotation by Stevan Davies The most significant and influential text of
the ancient Gnostic religion. 5½ x 8½, 208 pp, Quality PB, 978-1-59473-082-5 **$16.99**

JUDAISM

The Divine Feminine in Biblical Wisdom Literature
Selections Annotated & Explained
Translation & Annotation by Rabbi Rami Shapiro; Foreword by Rev. Cynthia Bourgeault, PhD
Uses the Hebrew Bible and Wisdom literature to explain Sophia's way of wisdom
and illustrate Her creative energy. 5½ x 8½, 240 pp, Quality PB, 978-1-59473-109-9 **$16.99**

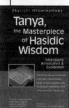

Ecclesiastes: Annotated & Explained
Translation & Annotation by Rabbi Rami Shapiro; Foreword by Rev. Barbara Cawthorne Crafton
A timeless teaching on living well amid uncertainty and insecurity.
5½ x 8½, 160 pp, Quality PB, 978-1-59473-287-4 **$16.99**

Ethics of the Sages: Pirke Avot—Annotated & Explained
Translation & Annotation by Rabbi Rami Shapiro Clarifies the ethical teachings of the
early Rabbis. 5½ x 8½, 192 pp, Quality PB, 978-1-59473-207-2 **$16.99**

Hasidic Tales: Annotated & Explained
Translation & Annotation by Rabbi Rami Shapiro; Foreword by Andrew Harvey
Introduces the legendary tales of the impassioned Hasidic rabbis, presenting them as
stories rather than as parables. 5½ x 8½, 240 pp, Quality PB, 978-1-893361-86-7 **$16.95**

The Hebrew Prophets: Selections Annotated & Explained
Translation & Annotation by Rabbi Rami Shapiro; Foreword by Rabbi Zalman M. Schachter-Shalomi
5½ x 8½, 224 pp, Quality PB, 978-1-59473-037-5 **$16.99**

Tanya, the Masterpiece of Hasidic Wisdom: Selections Annotated &
Explained *Translation & Annotation by Rabbi Rami Shapiro; Foreword by Rabbi Zalman M.
Schachter-Shalomi* Clarifies one of the most powerful and potentially transforma-
tive books of Jewish wisdom. 5½ x 8½, 240 pp, Quality PB, 978-1-59473-275-1 **$16.99**

Zohar: Annotated & Explained *Translation & Annotation by Daniel C. Matt;
Foreword by Andrew Harvey* The canonical text of Jewish mystical tradition.
5½ x 8½, 176 pp, Quality PB, 978-1-893361-51-5 **$15.99**

Sacred Texts—continued

MORMONISM

The Book of Mormon: Selections Annotated & Explained
Annotation by Jana Riess; Foreword by Phyllis Tickle Explores the sacred epic that is cherished by more than twelve million members of the LDS church as the keystone of their faith. 5½ x 8½, 272 pp, Quality PB, 978-1-59473-076-4 **$16.99**

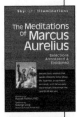

NATIVE AMERICAN

Native American Stories of the Sacred: Annotated & Explained
Retold & Annotated by Evan T. Pritchard These teaching tales contain elegantly simple illustrations of time-honored truths. 5½ x 8½, 272 pp, Quality PB, 978-1-59473-112-9 **$16.99**

STOICISM

The Meditations of Marcus Aurelius: Selections Annotated & Explained *Annotation by Russell McNeil, PhD; Translation by George Long, revised by Russell McNeil, PhD* Ancient Stoic wisdom that speaks vibrantly today about life, business, government and spirit. 5½ x 8½, 288 pp, Quality PB, 978-1-59473-236-2 **$16.99**

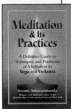

Hinduism / Vedanta

The Four Yogas: A Guide to the Spiritual Paths of Action, Devotion, Meditation and Knowledge *by Swami Adiswarananda*
6 x 9, 320 pp, Quality PB, 978-1-59473-223-2 **$19.99**; HC, 978-1-59473-143-3 **$29.99**

Meditation & Its Practices: A Definitive Guide to Techniques and Traditions of Meditation in Yoga and Vedanta *by Swami Adiswarananda* 6 x 9, 504 pp, Quality PB, 978-1-59473-105-1 **$24.99**

The Spiritual Quest and the Way of Yoga: The Goal, the Journey and the Milestones *by Swami Adiswarananda* 6 x 9, 288 pp, HC, 978-1-59473-113-6 **$29.99**

Sri Ramakrishna, the Face of Silence
by Swami Nikhilananda and Dhan Gopal Mukerji; Edited with an Introduction by Swami Adiswarananda; Foreword by Dhan Gopal Mukerji 6 x 9, 352 pp, Quality PB, 978-1-59473-233-1 **$21.99**

Sri Sarada Devi, The Holy Mother: Her Teachings and Conversations
Translated with Notes by Swami Nikhilananda; Edited with an Introduction by Swami Adiswarananda 6 x 9, 288 pp, HC, 978-1-59473-070-2 **$29.99**

The Vedanta Way to Peace and Happiness *by Swami Adiswarananda*
6 x 9, 240 pp, Quality PB, 978-1-59473-180-8 **$18.99**; HC, 978-1-59473-034-4 **$29.99**

Vivekananda, World Teacher: His Teachings on the Spiritual Unity of Humankind
Edited and with an Introduction by Swami Adiswarananda
6 x 9, 272 pp, Quality PB, 978-1-59473-210-2 **$21.99**

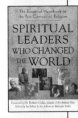

Sikhism

The First Sikh Spiritual Master: Timeless Wisdom from the Life and Teachings of Guru Nanak *by Harish Dhillon* 6 x 9, 192 pp, Quality PB, 978-1-59473-209-6 **$16.99**

Spiritual Biography

Spiritual Leaders Who Changed the World
The Essential Handbook to the Past Century of Religion
Edited by Ira Rifkin and the Editors at SkyLight Paths; Foreword by Dr. Robert Coles
An invaluable reference to the most important spiritual leaders of the past 100 years.
6 x 9, 304 pp, b/w photos, Quality PB, 978-1-59473-241-6 **$18.99**

Mahatma Gandhi: His Life and Ideas *by Charles F. Andrews; Foreword by Dr. Arun Gandhi*
Examines the religious ideas and political dynamics that influenced the birth of the peaceful resistance movement. 6 x 9, 336 pp, b/w photos, Quality PB, 978-1-893361-89-8 **$18.95**

Bede Griffiths: An Introduction to His Interspiritual Thought
by Wayne Teasdale The first study of his contemplative experience and thought, exploring the intersection of Hinduism and Christianity.
6 x 9, 288 pp, Quality PB, 978-1-893361-77-5 **$18.95**

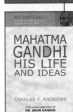

Spirituality

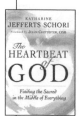

The Heartbeat of God: Finding the Sacred in the Middle of Everything
by Katharine Jefferts Schori; Foreword by Joan Chittister, OSB
Explores our connections to other people, to other nations and with the environ-
ment through the lens of faith. 6 x 9, 240 pp, HC, 978-1-59473-292-8 **$21.99**

A Dangerous Dozen: Twelve Christians Who Threatened the Status
Quo but Taught Us to Live Like Jesus
by the Rev. Canon C. K. Robertson, PhD; Foreword by Archbishop Desmond Tutu
Profiles twelve visionary men and women who challenged society and showed the
world a different way of living. 6 x 9, 208 pp, Quality PB, 978-1-59473-298-0 **$16.99**

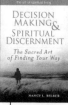

Decision Making & Spiritual Discernment: The Sacred Art of
Finding Your Way *by Nancy L. Bieber*
Presents three essential aspects of Spirit-led decision making: willingness, atten-
tiveness and responsiveness. 5½ x 8½, 208 pp, Quality PB, 978-1-59473-289-8 **$16.99**

Laugh Your Way to Grace: Reclaiming the Spiritual Power of Humor
by Rev. Susan Sparks A powerful, humorous case for laughter as a spiritual, healing
path. 6 x 9, 176 pp, Quality PB, 978-1-59473-280-5 **$16.99**

Living into Hope: A Call to Spiritual Action for Such a Time as This
by Rev. Dr. Joan Brown Campbell; Foreword by Karen Armstrong
A visionary minister speaks out on the pressing issues that face us today, offering
inspiration and challenge. 6 x 9, 208 pp, HC, 978-1-59473-283-6 **$21.99**

Claiming Earth as Common Ground: The Ecological Crisis through the Lens of Faith
by Andrea Cohen-Kiener; Foreword by Rev. Sally Bingham
6 x 9, 192 pp, Quality PB, 978-1-59473-261-4 **$16.99**

Bread, Body, Spirit: Finding the Sacred in Food
Edited and with Introductions by Alice Peck 6 x 9, 224 pp, Quality PB, 978-1-59473-242-3 **$19.99**

Creating a Spiritual Retirement: A Guide to the Unseen Possibilities in Our Lives
by Molly Srode 6 x 9, 208 pp, b/w photos, Quality PB, 978-1-59473-050-4 **$14.99**

Creative Aging: Rethinking Retirement and Non-Retirement in a Changing World
by Marjory Zoet Bankson 6 x 9, 160 pp, Quality PB, 978-1-59473-281-2 **$16.99**

Keeping Spiritual Balance as We Grow Older: More than 65 Creative Ways to
Use Purpose, Prayer, and the Power of Spirit to Build a Meaningful Retirement
by Molly and Bernie Srode 8 x 8, 224 pp, Quality PB, 978-1-59473-042-9 **$16.99**

Hearing the Call across Traditions: Readings on Faith and Service
Edited by Adam Davis; Foreword by Eboo Patel
6 x 9, 352 pp, Quality PB, 978-1-59473-303-1 **$18.99**; HC, 978-1-59473-264-5 **$29.99**

Honoring Motherhood: Prayers, Ceremonies & Blessings
Edited and with Introductions by Lynn L. Caruso 5 x 7¼, 272 pp, HC, 978-1-59473-239-3 **$19.99**

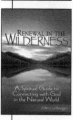

Journeys of Simplicity: Traveling Light with Thomas Merton, Bashō, Edward Abbey,
Annie Dillard & Others *by Philip Harnden*
5 x 7¼, 144 pp, Quality PB, 978-1-59473-181-5 **$12.99**; 128 pp, HC, 978-1-893361-76-8 **$16.95**

The Losses of Our Lives: The Sacred Gifts of Renewal in Everyday Loss
by Dr. Nancy Copeland-Payton 6 x 9, 192 pp, HC, 978-1-59473-271-3 **$19.99**

Renewal in the Wilderness: A Spiritual Guide to Connecting with God in the
Natural World *by John Lionberger*
6 x 9, 176 pp, b/w photos, Quality PB, 978-1-59473-219-5 **$16.99**

Soul Fire: Accessing Your Creativity
by Thomas Ryan, CSP 6 x 9, 160 pp, Quality PB, 978-1-59473-243-0 **$16.99**

A Spirituality for Brokenness: Discovering Your Deepest Self in Difficult Times
by Terry Taylor 6 x 9, 176 pp, Quality PB, 978-1-59473-229-4 **$16.99**

A Walk with Four Spiritual Guides: Krishna, Buddha, Jesus, and Ramakrishna
by Andrew Harvey 5½ x 8½, 192 pp, b/w photos & illus., Quality PB, 978-1-59473-138-9 **$15.99**

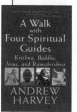

The Workplace and Spirituality: New Perspectives on Research and Practice
Edited by Dr. Joan Marques, Dr. Satinder Dhiman and Dr. Richard King
6 x 9, 256 pp, HC, 978-1-59473-260-7 **$29.99**

Spiritual Practice

Fly Fishing—The Sacred Art: Casting a Fly as a Spiritual Practice
by Rabbi Eric Eisenkramer and Rev. Michael Attas, MD
Illuminates what fly fishing can teach you about reflection, awe and wonder; the benefits of solitude; the blessing of community and the search for the Divine.
5½ x 8½, 192 pp (est), Quality PB, 978-1-59473-299-7 **$16.99**

Lectio Divina—The Sacred Art: Transforming Words & Images into Heart-Centered Prayer *by Christine Valters Paintner, PhD*
Expands the practice of sacred reading beyond scriptural texts and makes it accessible in contemporary life. 5½ x 8½, 240 pp, Quality PB, 978-1-59473-300-0 **$16.99**

Haiku—The Sacred Art: A Spiritual Practice in Three Lines
by Margaret D. McGee 5½ x 8½, 192 pp, Quality PB, 978-1-59473-269-0 **$16.99**

Dance—The Sacred Art: The Joy of Movement as a Spiritual Practice
by Cynthia Winton-Henry 5½ x 8½, 224 pp, Quality PB, 978-1-59473-268-3 **$16.99**

Spiritual Adventures in the Snow: Skiing & Snowboarding as Renewal for Your Soul *by Dr. Marcia McFee and Rev. Karen Foster; Foreword by Paul Arthur*
5½ x 8½, 208 pp, Quality PB, 978-1-59473-270-6 **$16.99**

Divining the Body: Reclaim the Holiness of Your Physical Self *by Jan Phillips*
8 x 8, 256 pp, Quality PB, 978-1-59473-080-1 **$16.99**

Everyday Herbs in Spiritual Life: A Guide to Many Practices
by Michael J. Caduto; Foreword by Rosemary Gladstar
7 x 9, 208 pp, 20+ b/w illus., Quality PB, 978-1-59473-174-7 **$16.99**

Giving—The Sacred Art: Creating a Lifestyle of Generosity
by Lauren Tyler Wright 5½ x 8½, 208 pp, Quality PB, 978-1-59473-224-9 **$16.99**

Hospitality—The Sacred Art: Discovering the Hidden Spiritual Power of Invitation and Welcome *by Rev. Nanette Sawyer; Foreword by Rev. Dirk Ficca*
5½ x 8½, 208 pp, Quality PB, 978-1-59473-228-7 **$16.99**

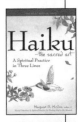

Labyrinths from the Outside In: Walking to Spiritual Insight—A Beginner's Guide
by Donna Schaper and Carole Ann Camp
6 x 9, 208 pp, b/w illus. and photos, Quality PB, 978-1-893361-18-8 **$16.95**

Practicing the Sacred Art of Listening: A Guide to Enrich Your Relationships and Kindle Your Spiritual Life *by Kay Lindahl* 8 x 8, 176 pp, Quality PB, 978-1-893361-85-0 **$16.95**

Recovery—The Sacred Art: The Twelve Steps as Spiritual Practice *by Rami Shapiro; Foreword by Joan Borysenko, PhD* 5½ x 8½, 240 pp, Quality PB, 978-1-59473-259-1 **$16.99**

Running—The Sacred Art: Preparing to Practice *by Dr. Warren A. Kay; Foreword by Kristin Armstrong* 5½ x 8½, 160 pp, Quality PB, 978-1-59473-227-0 **$16.99**

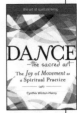

The Sacred Art of Chant: Preparing to Practice
by Ana Hernández 5½ x 8½, 192 pp, Quality PB, 978-1-59473-036-8 **$15.99**

The Sacred Art of Fasting: Preparing to Practice
by Thomas Ryan, CSP 5½ x 8½, 192 pp, Quality PB, 978-1-59473-078-8 **$15.99**

The Sacred Art of Forgiveness: Forgiving Ourselves and Others through God's Grace
by Marcia Ford 8 x 8, 176 pp, Quality PB, 978-1-59473-175-4 **$18.99**

The Sacred Art of Listening: Forty Reflections for Cultivating a Spiritual Practice
by Kay Lindahl; Illus. by Amy Schnapper 8 x 8, 160 pp, b/w illus., Quality PB, 978-1-893361-44-7 **$16.99**

The Sacred Art of Lovingkindness: Preparing to Practice
by Rabbi Rami Shapiro; Foreword by Marcia Ford 5½ x 8½, 176 pp, Quality PB, 978-1-59473-151-8 **$16.99**

Sacred Attention: A Spiritual Practice for Finding God in the Moment
by Margaret D. McGee 6 x 9, 144 pp, Quality PB, 978-1-59473-291-1 **$16.99**

Soul Fire: Accessing Your Creativity
by Thomas Ryan, CSP 6 x 9, 160 pp, Quality PB, 978-1-59473-243-0 **$16.99**

Thanking & Blessing—The Sacred Art: Spiritual Vitality through Gratefulness
by Jay Marshall, PhD; Foreword by Philip Gulley 5½ x 8½, 176 pp, Quality PB, 978-1-59473-231-7 **$16.99**

Women's Interest

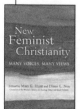

Spiritually Healthy Divorce: Navigating Disruption with Insight & Hope
by Carolyne Call
A spiritual map to help you move through the twists and turns of divorce.
6 x 9, 224 pp, Quality PB, 978-1-59473-288-1 **$16.99**

New Feminist Christianity: Many Voices, Many Views
Edited by Mary E. Hunt and Diann L. Neu
Insights from ministers and theologians, activists and leaders, artists and liturgists who are shaping the future. Taken together, their voices offer a starting point for building new models of religious life and worship.
6 x 9, 384 pp, HC, 978-1-59473-285-0 **$24.99**

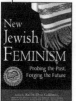

New Jewish Feminism: Probing the Past, Forging the Future
Edited by Rabbi Elyse Goldstein; Foreword by Anita Diamant
Looks at the growth and accomplishments of Jewish feminism and what they mean for Jewish women today and tomorrow. Features the voices of women from every area of Jewish life, addressing the important issues that concern Jewish women.
6 x 9, 480 pp, Quality PB, 978-1-58023-448-1 **$19.99**; HC, 978-1-58023-359-0 **$24.99***

Bread, Body, Spirit: Finding the Sacred in Food
Edited and with Introductions by Alice Peck
6 x 9, 224 pp, Quality PB, 978-1-59473-242-3 **$19.99**

Dance—The Sacred Art: The Joy of Movement as a Spiritual Practice
by Cynthia Winton-Henry 5½ x 8½, 224 pp, Quality PB, 978-1-59473-268-3 **$16.99**

Daughters of the Desert: Stories of Remarkable Women from Christian, Jewish and Muslim Traditions
by Claire Rudolf Murphy, Meghan Nuttall Sayres, Mary Cronk Farrell, Sarah Conover and Betsy Wharton
5½ x 8½, 192 pp, Illus., Quality PB, 978-1-59473-106-8 **$14.99** Inc. reader's discussion guide

The Divine Feminine in Biblical Wisdom Literature
Selections Annotated & Explained
Translation & Annotation by Rabbi Rami Shapiro; Foreword by Rev. Cynthia Bourgeault, PhD
5½ x 8½, 240 pp, Quality PB, 978-1-59473-109-9 **$16.99**

Divining the Body: Reclaim the Holiness of Your Physical Self
by Jan Phillips 8 x 8, 256 pp, Quality PB, 978-1-59473-080-1 **$16.99**

Honoring Motherhood: Prayers, Ceremonies & Blessings
Edited and with Introductions by Lynn L. Caruso 5 x 7¼, 272 pp, HC, 978-1-59473-239-3 **$19.99**

Next to Godliness: Finding the Sacred in Housekeeping
Edited by Alice Peck 6 x 9, 224 pp, Quality PB, 978-1-59473-214-0 **$19.99**

ReVisions: Seeing Torah through a Feminist Lens
by Rabbi Elyse Goldstein 5½ x 8½, 224 pp, Quality PB, 978-1-58023-117-6 **$16.95***

The Triumph of Eve & Other Subversive Bible Tales
by Matt Biers-Ariel 5½ x 8½, 192 pp, Quality PB, 978-1-59473-176-1 **$14.99**

White Fire: A Portrait of Women Spiritual Leaders in America
by Malka Drucker; Photos by Gay Block 7 x 10, 320 pp, b/w photos, HC, 978-1-893361-64-5 **$24.95**

Woman Spirit Awakening in Nature
Growing Into the Fullness of Who You Are
by Nancy Barrett Chickerneo, PhD; Foreword by Eileen Fisher
8 x 8, 224 pp, b/w illus., Quality PB, 978-1-59473-250-8 **$16.99**

Women of Color Pray: Voices of Strength, Faith, Healing, Hope and Courage
Edited and with Introductions by Christal M. Jackson
5 x 7¼, 208 pp, Quality PB, 978-1-59473-077-1 **$15.99**

The Women's Torah Commentary: New Insights from Women Rabbis on the 54 Weekly Torah Portions *Edited by Rabbi Elyse Goldstein*
6 x 9, 496 pp, Quality PB, 978-1-58023-370-5 **$19.99**; HC, 978-1-58023-076-6 **$34.95***

* A book from Jewish Lights, SkyLight Paths' sister imprint

Prayer / Meditation

Sacred Attention: A Spiritual Practice for Finding God in the Moment
by Margaret D. McGee
Framed on the Christian liturgical year, this inspiring guide explores ways to develop a practice of attention as a means of talking—and listening—to God.
6 x 9, 144 pp, Quality PB, 978-1-59473-291-1 **$16.99**

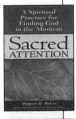

Women of Color Pray: Voices of Strength, Faith, Healing, Hope and Courage
Edited and with Introductions by Christal M. Jackson
Through these prayers, poetry, lyrics, meditations and affirmations, you will share in the strong and undeniable connection women of color share with God.
5 x 7¼, 208 pp, Quality PB, 978-1-59473-077-1 **$15.99**

Secrets of Prayer: A Multifaith Guide to Creating Personal Prayer in Your Life   *by Nancy Corcoran, CSJ*
This compelling, multifaith guidebook offers you companionship and encouragement on the journey to a healthy prayer life. 6 x 9, 160 pp, Quality PB, 978-1-59473-215-7 **$16.99**

Prayers to an Evolutionary God
by William Cleary; Afterword by Diarmuid O'Murchu
Inspired by the spiritual and scientific teachings of Diarmuid O'Murchu and Teilhard de Chardin, reveals that religion and science can be combined to create an expanding view of the universe—an evolutionary faith.
6 x 9, 208 pp, HC, 978-1-59473-006-1 **$21.99**

The Art of Public Prayer, 2nd Edition: Not for Clergy Only
by Lawrence A. Hoffman, PhD 6 x 9, 288 pp, Quality PB, 978-1-893361-06-5 **$19.99**

A Heart of Stillness: A Complete Guide to Learning the Art of Meditation
by David A. Cooper 5½ x 8½, 272 pp, Quality PB, 978-1-893361-03-4 **$18.99**

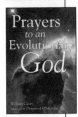

Meditation without Gurus: A Guide to the Heart of Practice
by Clark Strand 5½ x 8½, 192 pp, Quality PB, 978-1-893361-93-5 **$16.95**

Praying with Our Hands: 21 Practices of Embodied Prayer from the World's Spiritual Traditions *by Jon M. Sweeney; Photos by Jennifer J. Wilson; Foreword by Mother Tessa Bielecki; Afterword by Taitetsu Unno, PhD*
8 x 8, 96 pp, 22 duotone photos, Quality PB, 978-1-893361-16-4 **$16.95**

Three Gates to Meditation Practice: A Personal Journey into Sufism, Buddhism, and Judaism   *by David A. Cooper* 5½ x 8½, 240 pp, Quality PB, 978-1-893361-22-5 **$16.95**

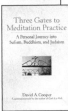

Prayer / M. Basil Pennington, OCSO

Finding Grace at the Center, 3rd Edition: The Beginning of Centering Prayer   *with Thomas Keating, OCSO, and Thomas E. Clarke, SJ; Foreword by Rev. Cynthia Bourgeault, PhD* A practical guide to a simple and beautiful form of meditative prayer. 5 x 7¼, 128 pp, Quality PB, 978-1-59473-182-2 **$12.99**

The Monks of Mount Athos: A Western Monk's Extraordinary Spiritual Journey on Eastern Holy Ground *Foreword by Archimandrite Dionysios*
Explores the landscape, monastic communities and food of Athos.
6 x 9, 352 pp, Quality PB, 978-1-893361-78-2 **$18.95**

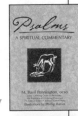

Psalms: A Spiritual Commentary *Illus. by Phillip Ratner*
Reflections on some of the most beloved passages from the Bible's most widely read book.   6 x 9, 176 pp, 24 full-page b/w illus., Quality PB, 978-1-59473-234-8 **$16.99**

The Song of Songs: A Spiritual Commentary *Illus. by Phillip Ratner*
Explore the Bible's most challenging mystical text.
6 x 9, 160 pp, 14 full-page b/w illus., Quality PB, 978-1-59473-235-5 **$16.99**
HC, 978-1-59473-004-7 **$19.99**

About SKYLIGHT PATHS Publishing

SkyLight Paths Publishing is creating a place where people of different spiritual traditions come together for challenge and inspiration, a place where we can help each other understand the mystery that lies at the heart of our existence.

Through spirituality, our religious beliefs are increasingly becoming a part of our lives—rather than *apart* from our lives. While many of us may be more interested than ever in spiritual growth, we may be less firmly planted in traditional religion. Yet, we do want to deepen our relationship to the sacred, to learn from our own as well as from other faith traditions, and to practice in new ways.

SkyLight Paths sees both believers and seekers as a community that increasingly transcends traditional boundaries of religion and denomination—people wanting to learn from each other, *walking together, finding the way.*

For your information and convenience, at the back of this book we have provided a list of other SkyLight Paths books you might find interesting and useful. They cover the following subjects:

Buddhism / Zen	Global Spiritual	Monasticism
Catholicism	Perspectives	Mysticism
Children's Books	Gnosticism	Poetry
Christianity	Hinduism /	Prayer
Comparative	Vedanta	Religious Etiquette
Religion	Inspiration	Retirement
Current Events	Islam / Sufism	Spiritual Biography
Earth-Based	Judaism	Spiritual Direction
Spirituality	Kabbalah	Spirituality
Enneagram	Meditation	Women's Interest
	Midrash Fiction	Worship

Or phone, fax, mail or e-mail to: SKYLIGHT PATHS Publishing
Sunset Farm Offices, Route 4 • P.O. Box 237 • Woodstock, Vermont 05091
Tel: (802) 457-4000 • Fax: (802) 457-4004 • www.skylightpaths.com
Credit card orders: (800) 962-4544 (8:30AM–5:30PM ET Monday–Friday)
Generous discounts on quantity orders. SATISFACTION GUARANTEED. Prices subject to change.